ANCIENT LIVES OF SCOTTISH SAINTS

PART TWO
KENTIGERN BY JOCELIN, SERVANUS, MARGARET BY TURGOT, AND MAGNUS.

translated by
W. M. Metcalfe

First published in 1895
FACSIMILE REPRINT 1998
by LLANERCH PUBLISHERS,
FELINFACH.

ISBN 1 86143 054 X

CONTENTS.

S. KENTIGERN BY JOCELIN, A MONK OF FURNESS,   ·   ·   · 175

S. SERVANUS, ·   ·   ·   ·   ·   ·   ·   · 281

S. MARGARET, QUEEN OF SCOTLAND, BY TURGOT,   ·   ·   · 295

S. MAGNUS, ·   ·   ·   ·   ·   ·   ·   · 323

INDEX, ·   ·   ·   ·   ·   ·   ·   · 367

ERRATA.

,, 251, ,, 22 ,,   ,, " opprobium " read, " opprobrium."

,, 283, ,, 20 ,,   ,, " dragon " read " drake."

LIFE OF S. KENTIGERN.

TO his most reverend lord and dearest father, Jocelin, the
anointed of the Lord Jesus Christ, Jocelin, the least
of the poor of Christ, animated and sustained by filial love
and obedience, wishes the salvation of body and soul in our
Saviour.

Since your great name, high office, and equal judgment,
your life untarnished by any breath of evil fame, and your long
tried religion, persuade me, after most careful consideration,
that you love the beauty of the House of the Lord over which
you preside, I have deemed it fitting to present to you the first
fruits of my gleanings, which are redolent of the beauty and
glory both of yourself and your Church. For, according to
your command, I have wandered through the streets and lanes
of the city seeking a record of the life of S. Kentigern, in whom
your soul delights, and in whose chair the grace of Divine
condescension, by the adoption of sons, by ecclesiastical election, and by succession of ministry, has caused your sanctity
to preside. Wherefore I sought diligently for a life of him, if
perchance one might be found, which seemed to be supported
with greater authority and more evident truth, and to be
written in a more graceful style than the one which your
Church has hitherto used, because that, as it seems to many, is
stained throughout, being discoloured by an uncouth diction,
and obscured by an uncultivated style; and, what above all
these things a wise man would still more abhor, in the very

beginning of the narrative there are matters which are manifestly contrary to sound doctrine and the Catholic Faith.   But
another little volume I have found, written in the Celtic
dialect, which, though abounding from beginning to end with
solecisms, contains the life and acts of the holy pontiff at
greater length.   Seeing the life of so precious a pontiff,
glorious with signs and wonders, and most illustrious in virtues
and doctrine, perversely narrated and marred by unsound
doctrine, or greatly obscured by barbaric language, I confess I
was grieved and took it ill.   I resolved, therefore, to put
together the materials I had collected from either volume for
its restoration, and as far as I could, and in obedience to your
command, season what had been rudely composed with Roman
salt.   It is absurd, I think, that so precious a treasure should
be swathed in such vile wrappages, and I have endeavoured,
therefore, to cover it, if not with tissues of gold or silk, at least
with pure linen.   I have attempted, moreover, to so pour the
life-giving liquid from the old vessel into the new, that, drawing it out according to the scanty capacity of the vessel, it may
be acceptable to the more simple, and neither useless to those
of moderate ability, nor contemptible to those who are more
richly endowed.   Assisted, therefore, by the prayers and
merits of our holy President, if the favour of the Inspirer
from on High, encourage me, I shall so temper my style that
the work I have undertaken shall not be obscured by creeping
in the darkness through poverty of language, nor swell with
rhetorical phrases beyond what is fitting, through aiming too
high, lest I should seem to have planted a grove in the temple
of the Lord contrary to His command.   Hence the whole aim
of this work, all the fruit of my labour, ought, it has seemed to
me, to be consecrated to your name and to be submitted for
your consideration.   If, however, any thing inelegant or insipid
be put forth, let it be seasoned with the salt of your discretion ;
if by chance there be anything in it which sounds scarcely
consonant with the truth, though I do not think there is, let it
be shaped and adjusted to the rule of your judgment.   But if
nothing be found in it failing in either of these respects, let it
be supported by your testimony and confirmed by your

authority. And in all these things, if any thing come to light proceeding from my pen otherwise than becoming the subject, let it be imputed to the slenderness of my skill. And if any thing appear in it worthy of being read, let it be ascribed to your Eminency. Of the translation of this Saint, or of the miracles he performed after his death, I have been unable anywhere to find an account ; they either have not been recorded, because they have escaped the memory of those who were present, or they have been multiplied beyond enumeration and have been omitted, that the multitude of facts collected might not weary feeble readers. May your sanctity always live and flourish in the Lord.

Here ends the Prologue.

CHAPTER I.

Here beginneth the Life of S. Kentigern, Bishop and Confessor.

THE beginning of the record of the glorious life of the most illustrious Kentigern, very dear to God and men, a Nazarite of our Nazarene Jesus Christ, is consecrated by the divine oracle in which the Lord, anticipating in His gracious benedictions the blessed prophet Jeremiah, foretells that he should be a vessel of election sanctified to the work of his ministry, by such praise as this : " Before I formed thee in the belly I knew thee, and before thou camest forth out of the womb I sanctified thee and gave thee a prophet unto the nations." Truly the blessed Kentigern, who was known to God before he was born into the world, and bedewed with the grace of election before he came forth from his mother's womb, was made great by miracles before he became great either in his members or his merits. For him who was sanctified, and was to be yet more sanctified, the Holy of Holies Himself, while he was still shut up within the gates of the maternal womb, began to cause to shine forth in his very beginning the splendour of His virtues, that he might prove that the special gift of the Holy Ghost is not constrained by the chain of original sin. This man, I say, famous for his race and beauty, and distinguished in many ways by signs, and prodigies, and presages, was, by a decree of the Redeemer, destined to be a prophet, yea, also a teacher and chief ruler, to many nations.

Wherefore this most holy man, though he drew his original germ from a royal stem, came forth as a rose from the thorn, as a sweet smelling tree from filthy ground, since his mother was the daughter of a certain King, very pagan in his creed, a ruling prince in the northern parts of Britain. But when the sound of the preaching of the Christian Faith went forth in the land of that region, and the words of holy preachers advanced into those northern confines, whence every evil used to be spread, she heard with her ears those things which were to be heard, how the Brightness of the Eternal Light, the Sun of Righteousness, having risen by the Star of Virginity, illumined the world with the rays of His knowledge and love, and proclaimed salvation to them that were near and to them that were afar off, leading His own into all the fulness of the truth more efficaciously by the arguments of manifest signs ; then her heart burned within her, and in her meditation that fire burned which the Lord sent upon the earth, and she earnestly desired that it should be kindled. Her soul thirsting to come to the knowledge of the truth, she received the engrafted word which was able to save her soul from everlasting death. Though not yet washed in the water of the saving laver, she was nevertheless running in the way of the commandments of God with an enlarged and diligent heart.' She persevered continually in frequent almsgiving, in devout prayers, in learning the faith of the Church and in practising its discipline, as far as she might, for fear of her pagan father. With special devotion, however, did she, among these things, admire the fruitful purity of the Virgin Mother ; through admiring, she venerated, and, through venerating and loving, she desired to imitate it, and with a certain presumptuous boldness of feminine rashness, she desired to be like her in conceiving and in giving birth, and on this account she earnestly laboured to entreat the Lord.

After the lapse of some time she was found to be with child, and her soul magnified the Lord, believing in her simplicity that her desire had been accomplished. That, however, which was born in her she received from the embrace of man, but, as she often asserted, binding herself by an oath, by whom, or when, or in what way she conceived, she was unconscious. But though the fact of this secret was hid from her, or had escaped her memory, the truth of the matter ought by no means to perish from the mind of any discreet person, nor should any scruple arise from it. For though at present we bury in silence things which we find recorded in poetic songs or in histories which are not canonical, when we turn to the Sacred Volumes we read in the Book of Genesis that the daughters of Lot not only secretly stole for themselves their father's embraces, but also that each of them conceived by him when he was drunk, and entirely unwitting of the fact. It is certain, moreover, that many, through taking the draught of oblivion, which physicists call Letargion, have slept ; and when they suffered incisions in their members, and sometimes burning and abrasion in vital parts, have not in the least felt it, but have been ignorant, when awakened, of the things which were done to them. We frequently have heard that maidenly chastity has been stormed by tricks of jugglers, and that the deflowered has never known her deflowerer. It may be that something of the sort happened to this girl by the secret judg-ment of God, that she might not feel the mixture of the sexes, and so, when impregnated, might think herself undefiled.

We do not think that this has been mentioned here in vain, because the foolish and stupid people who live in the diocese of S. Kentigern do not shrink from asserting even that he was conceived and born of a virgin. But why should we delay with these things ? Indeed, we deem it both absurd and irrelevant to inquire further who the sower was, or how he ploughed or sowed the land, when the Lord, bestowing His favour, the land brought forth good and rich fruit—the fruit, I say, of this land which received a blessing from the Lord, whereby many generations are blessed by the Lord and receive from Him the fruit of eternal salvation. Meanwhile the woman went about,

and the signs of her seduction were apparent to all. . . . .
. . . .
When her condition was made known to the King, her father,
. . . .
he began more earnestly to try to learn from her—now urging her
with terrors, now coaxing her with blandishments—who had
caused her to be with child. But she, interposing with an oath in
the name of Christ, protested that she was innocent of all intercourse with man. But the King hearing this, and moved with
a more vehement rage, both because of the name of Christ,
which had been uttered by her mouth, and because he could
not find out the violator of his daughter, swore, and resolved to
keep his righteous judgment, that he would not in any respect
swerve from the law ordained by his ancestors in such matters
for the love or life of his own daughter.

CHAPTER II.

*Of the law established in those days among the Cambrian people
concerning Girls who committed fornication.*

THERE was among that barbarous people a law, promulgated
of old, that a girl who committed fornication in her father's
house, and was found with child, should be cast down from the
top of the highest mountain, and that her paramour should be
beheaded. Similarly among the ancient Saxons, almost down
to these modern times, the law continued that every virgin
deflowered of her own will in her father's house should, without
any remission, be buried alive, and her violator be hanged over
her tomb. What shall we say to these things, or what can we
conjecture concerning them? If such zeal for chastity burn in
the heathen, who are ignorant of the divine law, solely for the
sake of integrity, and out of respect for the traditions of their
fathers, what shall the Christian do who is constrained to the
preservation of chastity by the divine law, which promises as
the reward of it the joy of heaven, and likewise, on the other
hand, metes out for the transgression of it eternal punishment?

Behold, both sexes and every condition are now plunged in
every slough of carnal pollution almost as boldly as willingly,
because with impunity; and not only is the vilest herd polluted with the contagion, but those who are maintained by
ecclesiastical benefices and attached to divine offices deem
themselves happier, the more filthy they are. But now the
Hammerer of the whole earth, even the Spirit of Fornication, passes through them.   They who exhibit outwardly a
certain fancied form of godliness, but deny the power thereof
by their works, paying allegiance to this present world, are
known by their impure life to lie before God by their sacred
habit and tonsure.   Verily they ought to fear that which the
Lord threatens by His prophet, saying : " He who hath done
iniquity in the land of the saints shall not look upon the glory
of God."   Even now what is to be bewailed with every river
of tears?   That sin of sins, which is now committed with
impunity, than which nothing more detestable can be conceived, on account of which the sulphurous flame, a heavenly
judgment, destroyed the guilty in the Five Cities of the Plain.
Nor can he easily be found who will willingly reprove the
perpetrator.   For if any one, however rarely, be found whom
the zeal of the Lord's house consumeth, and who burneth with
the love of justice and integrity, so that he should seem to
censure such monstrous sins, he is straightway resisted to his
face as a sycophant, and denounced by all as a traducer ; his
mouth is closed, as of one speaking wickedly, his tongue is
decreed to be tied up.

Why is this?   Plainly because the body of Leviathan, as it
is written, is shut close up with scales, pressing upon one
another, and the shadows cover his shadow; because the crimin-
ous and guilty, who are members of the devil, are mutually
protected by others who labour in the same vice, that the
arrow of correction cannot pierce them.   Verily, as I think,
this is done as a proof of their inexcusable damnation, that
such men, being given over to a reprobate mind, neither receive
nor accept the rod of correction.   And the multitude, labouring in the same vice, mitigates not in the least their punishment because the many, not less than they themselves,

individually burn, as if cast into a furnace. But what shall we say of those on whom the duty is conjoined of binding and loosing, of shutting and opening, who are placed upon a candlestick, that in the House of the Lord they may shine by word and example? Do not the greater number in the present represent smoke rather than flame, and stench rather than brightness? Are they not dumb dogs, not able, yea, not willing, to bark? When they see manners more than bestial, they do not dare to rebuke them, especially since they themselves are conformed to their habits, yea, are worse deformed. For, as the people, so the priest; as the subject, so the prelate; yea, as the first in dignity, so the worse in iniquity, and they who excel in office excel also in vice. What the Scripture mystically says of such is to be feared for them : " If so much as a beast touch the mountain, it shall be stoned." The beast touches the mountain when any one of bestial life mounts to the chair of prelacy, and lays an impure hand on purifying sacrifices. Yet such is he who is commanded to be stoned, since it is clearly taught in the opinions of the holy Fathers that he ought to be subjected to a hard and heavy condemnation. That I have said these things by way of digression will, I trust, be burdensome to none. The zeal of this pagan man who spared not his own daughter, but for the fault of simple fornication delivered her to such a doom, ought to cause great shame to the worshippers of Christ to the planting and propagating of modesty.

CHAPTER III.

How the divine favour delivered the mother of S. Kentigern from the precipice and from shipwreck.

ACCORDINGLY the aforesaid girl was led by the command of the King to the summit of a very high mountain, called Dumpelder, in order that she might be cast down from thence and be broken limb from limb or dashed to pieces. But she, groaning heavily, and looking up to heaven, said in complaining words: "Justly do I suffer this, because I have acted as one of the foolish women, desiring to be equalled to the most holy, most serene Bearer of Salvation, the parent who brought forth her Father. But I beseech thee, O Lady! blessed among women, take away the iniquity of thine handmaid, for I have done very foolishly. O Mother of mercy! show the light of thy compassion towards me, and deliver me from the oppression which surrounds me. I beseech thee, O Lady, that as He, the Flower of the Angelic Mountains, without injury to thy snow white purity, vouchsaved ·to become in thee, the lowly valley, fertile in every virtue, the lily of our valleys, and as out of thee, the most firm mountain of the faith, the stone was hewn without hands, which grew into a great mountain and filled the whole earth ; so me, thine handmaid, though not yet washed in the sacred laver, yet firmly believing in thy Son, and hoping in the shadow of thy wings, do thou deliver from the imminent precipice, that the blessed name of thy Son may for ever be magnified in the sight of these people. Moreover, the offspring which I bear in my womb I promise to thy Son and to thee as a peculiar possession, to be thy servant all the days of his life."

When she had prayed in this manner with devout heart and mouth, the servants of the King cast her, continually invoking Christ and His mother, down from the top of the mountain. Then a thing, wonderful and unheard of from the past, occurred. When she fell she was not bruised, because the Lord supported her hand, therefore she felt no hurt. As it seemed to her, she descended to the earth like a winged bird, with a gentle gliding, lest, perchance, she should dash her foot against a stone. Thanksgiving and the voice of praise sound in the mouth of many who beheld these wonderful works of God. The holy and terrible name of Christ is magnified. The innocent is judged both to be deemed free from all further punishment, and in every way to be held in reverence. But, on the other hand, the idolaters and adversaries of the Christian Faith ascribed this miracle not to divine virtue but to magical arts ; and with unanimous voice proclaimed her a witch and a sorceress. Therefore there was a division among the people

concerning her.   Some said : " She is a good woman and
innocent."   Others said : " Nay, but by her artifices she
deceiveth the people, changeth her countenance, and deludeth
their senses."   The crowd, therefore, in the whirl of its own
words confused itself ; but the sacrilegious multitude prevailing, they moved the King, who was wholly given up to idolatry,
to pronounce a new judgment concerning his daughter.   At
length, by the general connivance of the assembly of the
wicked and of those who oppose the name of Christ, it was
decreed that the little pregnant woman should be placed alone
in a boat and exposed on the sea.   In order, therefore, that the
sentence thus resolved upon might be carried out, the servants
of the King embarked and took her far out to sea, and there,
placed alone in a very little boat of hides, put together after
the manner of the Irish, they committed her to fortune without a single oar, and then rowed back to the shore, and related
what they had done to the King and the people, who were
awaiting the issue of the event.   But these, mocking, said :
" She calls herself the handmaid of Christ.   She professes that
she has His power as her protector.   Let us see if her words
are true.   She trusteth in Christ, let Him deliver her, if He is
able, from the hand of death and from the peril of the sea."
   But the girl, destitute of all human help, commits herself to
Him alone who made the sea and the dry land, devoutly beseeching that He who had already saved her from the precipice
would save her from the imminent peril.   Wonderful to relate
—but with God nothing is impossible—that little boat in which
the pregnant girl was detained, ploughed the watery vortices
and the eddies of the waves towards the opposite shore in a
much swifter course than if it had been borne onward by a
wind filling the sails or propelled by the effort of many rowers.
For He who preserved Jonah the prophet unhurt amid the
whirlpools of the ocean when swallowed up in the huge belly
of the whale, who likewise by His right hand upheld the
blessed Peter when walking upon the waves that he might not
sink, and delivered his co-Apostle, who thrice suffered shipwreck, from the depths of the sea, brought the woman safe to
a haven of safety, for the sake of the child whom she bore in

her womb, whom He predestinated to be a chief steersman of
His own ship, that is, an excellent teacher and ruler of His
Church.

CHAPTER IV.

Of the birth of S. Kentigern, and of his education with S. Serf.

THE aforesaid woman landed on the sand near to a place
called Culross. In this place S. Serf was then dwelling, and
teaching many boys, who were to be trained to the Divine service, and in sacred literature. When she had landed on the shore,
the pangs of labour at once took hold upon her. Raising her
eyes, she saw afar off, though in the darkness, the sign of the
ashes of a fire near the shore, which, perhaps, some shepherds
or fishermen had left. She therefore crawled to the place, and
as best she could kindled for herself a fire. But when the
dawn, the harbinger of the divine light, began to whiten, the
time was fulfilled that she should be delivered. And she
brought forth a son, about to be a herald and messenger of the
true Light.

Now, at the same hour, S. Serf, while intent upon prayer
after Mass in the morning matins, and drawing in his breath
with the sweetness of holy contemplation, heard the angelic
companies chanting their sweet praises on high, and rejoicing together with them in their praises, he with his disciples exulted
and eagerly offered in spirit to the Lord the sacrifices of jubila-
tion by singing : " We Praise Thee, O Lord." The clerics were
astonished at the novelty of the event, and when they inquired
what had happened, he told them all in order the whole matter, and the hymning of the angels, and sedulously exhorted
them that they themselves should offer the calves of their lips
to the Lord. But there were in the neighbourhood shepherds
keeping watch over their flocks by night, and they going forth
at the break of day, when they saw a fire burning close at
hand, made haste and came to it, and found the young woman

newly delivered of a child, and the infant wrapped in rags and
lying in the open air. They were moved with pity, took care
of them by increasing the fire and supplying them with food,
and by obtaining other necessaries; and bringing them in as
suitable a way as they could, they presented them to S. Serf,
and rehearsed the matter to him in order.

When he heard these things, and saw the little boy, the .
mouth of the blessed old man was filled with spiritual laughter,
and his heart with joy. Wherefore also in the language of his
country he exclaimed: "Mochohe! Mochohe!" which in Latin
means "Care mi, Care mi," adding: "Blessed art thou who
hast come in the name of the Lord." He therefore took them
to his dwelling, nourished and educated them as if they had
been his own kindred. Accordingly, after certain days had
elapsed, he bathed them in the laver of regeneration and re-
novation, and anointed them with the sacred chrism; calling
the mother Taneu, and the boy Kyentyern, which, being
interpreted, is The Capital Lord. That this new name with
which the mouth of S. Serf named him was not received in
vain shall be clearly set forth in its place in the following
pages. Therefore the man of the Lord educated the child of
the Lord, like another Samuel, commended and assigned to
him by God. The child grew and waxed strong, and the grace
of God was with him. But when the age of understanding
and the time fit and acceptable for learning came, he delivered
him to be instructed in letters, and, that he might profit in
these things, spent much labour and care upon him. Nor was
he in this respect defrauded of his desire; for the boy, in
acquiring and retaining, responded well and richly to his
training, like a tree which is planted near the running waters,
which bringeth forth its fruit in due season. The boy
advanced, the unction of a good hope and a holy disposition
teaching him, in the discipline of letters, and not less in the
exercises of the sacred virtues. For there were bestowed upon
him by the Father of Lights, from Whom cometh down every
good and every perfect gift, a docile heart, a mind quick to
understand, a memory tenacious in retaining what he had
learnt, a tongue persuasive in setting forth what he willed; a

voice, high, sweet, harmonious, and almost unwearied, in singing the divine praises. A praiseworthy life gilded all these gifts of grace, and therefore beyond all his companions he was precious and beloved in the eyes of the holy old man. Wherefore, also, he was accustomed to call him, in the language of his country, Mungher, which in Latin means Karissimus Amicus ; and by this name, down to the present day, the common people are frequently used to call him, and to invoke him in their necessities.

CHAPTER V.

Of the little bird which was killed and then restored to life by Kentigern.

THE fellow pupils of S. Kentigern, seeing that he was loved by their teacher and spiritual father more than all the rest, hated him, nor could' they say anything peaceably to him either publicly or in private. Wherefore in many ways they lay in wait for him, abused, envied, and slandered him. But the child of the Lord always had the eyes of his heart towards the Lord, and grieved more for them than for himself, caring little for all the unjust machinations of men. Now, a little bird, which on account of the redness of its body is called the redbreast, by the will of the Heavenly Father, without whom not one sparrow falleth to the ground, was wont to receive its daily food from the hand of Serf, the servant of God, and in consequence of this had become familiar and at home with him. Sometimes it was even wont to rest upon his head, or face, or shoulder, or in his bosom, or to sit by his side as he prayed or read ; and by the flapping of its wings, or by the sound of its inarticulate voice, or by some other little gesture, it showed the affection which it had for him. So that sometimes the face of the man of God assumed the joy which was shadowed forth in the motion of the bird, as he wondered at the great power of the Creator in this little creature, to Whom the dumb speak, and irrational things are known to have understanding.

And because this bird frequently, at the command or beck of the man of God, came to him or departed from him, it brought to light the unbelief and hardness of heart of his disciples, and showed clearly their disobedience. Let not this seem strange to any one, seeing that the Lord, by the voice of an animal dumb and a beast of burden, reproved the foolishness of the prophet ; and Solomon, the wisest of men, sends the sluggard to the ant, that, by considering its labour and industry, he may shake off his torpor and sloth. Moreover, a holy and wise man called his religious to consider the work of the bees, that in their little bodies they might learn the beautiful discipline of service. But perhaps it will seem marvellous to some that a man so holy and perfect should take delight in the play or ways of a little bird. But let such know that perfect men ought at times to have the severity of their discipline mitigated by something of this kind, in order that they who mentally rise up to God may at times lower themselves to us ; because even the bow requires occasionally to be unbent from its daily strain, lest at the needful time it be found nerveless and useless for the discharge of the arrow. For birds in passing through the air rise with outstretched wings, and again closing them, descend to the lower parts of the earth.

Therefore on a certain day, when the aged man entered his oratory to offer up to God the incense of prayers, the boys took advantage of his absence, and began to indulge in play with the aforesaid little bird ; and, while they handled it among themselves, and tried to snatch it from each other, it died in their hands, and its head was torn from its body. When this was done, their play was changed into sorrow, and they already, in imagination, saw the strokes of the rods which are wont to be the greatest torment of boys, hanging over them. At length, having taken counsel among themselves, they laid the blame on the boy Kentigern, who had kept himself entirely aloof from the affair, and they showed him the dead bird, and threw it from them before the old man arrived. The old man took the destruction of the bird very ill, and threatened to avenge its death upon its destroyer very severely. The boys, therefore, rejoiced, thinking that they had escaped, and that they had turned on Kentigern the punishment due to themselves, and that they had lessened the grace of friendship which Serf had hitherto entertained towards him.

When Kentigern, the most pure child, learned this, he took the bird into his hands, put the head to the body, and impressed upon it the sign of the cross, and raising his pure hands in prayer to the Lord, said: "O Lord Jesus Christ, in whose hand is the breath of all Thy creatures, rational and irrational, give back to this little bird the breath of life, that Thy blessed name may be glorified for ever." These words spake the Saint in prayer, and immediately the bird was restored to life ; and not only rose safely with untrammelled flight in the air, but flew forth in its usual way to meet the old man with joy as he returned from the church. On seeing this prodigy the heart of the holy old man exulted in the Lord, and his soul magnified the child of the Lord in the Lord, and the Lord who alone doeth marvellous works, and was working in the child. By this remarkable sign, therefore, the Lord signified, nay, in a way presignified, Kentigern to be His own, and began to announce him whom He afterwards, and in manifold ways, made more remarkable by wonders.

CHAPTER VI.

Of the fire put out through envy by the companions of S. Kentigern and by his breath brought down from heaven on a little branch of hazel.

IT was a rule with S. Serf that each of the boys whom he trained and instructed should, during the course of the week, carefully attend to arrange the lamps in the church while the divine office was being celebrated there by day and by night, and that for this purpose, when the rest had gone to sleep, one of them should diligently attend to the fire, lest any neglect should occur in the divine service on account of the want of light. It came to pass that S. Kentigern was appointed to this service in the order of his course, and while he was performing it diligently and in order, his rivals, inflamed with the torches of envy, yea, blinded, as it is the way with the perverse to envy the progress of their betters, and to persecute or prevent or depreciate the good in others which they do not, or will not, or can not have in themselves, secretly on a certain solemn night extinguished all the fire within the habitations of the monastery and the places in its neighbourhood; and then, as if ignorant and innocent sought their couches. And when about cockcrow, Kentigern rose according to custom at the sacred vigils, in order that, as custom required, he might attend to the lights, he sought for fire all around and found none.

At length, becoming aware of the wickedness of his rivals, he determined to give place to envy, and began to leave the monastery. And when he came to the hedge which surrounded that habitation, he came to himself and stood still, and armed his soul to endure perils among false brethren and to bear the persecution of the froward. Then returning to the house, he laid hold of and drew out a branch of a growing hazel which had come up beside the hedge, and, animated by faith, besought the Father of Lights to lighten his darkness by the pouring in of new light, and in a new way prepare a lamp for him by which he might clothe with wholesome confusion his enemies who were persecuting him. Therefore, raising his pure hand, he made upon the branch the sign of the cross, and blessing it in the name of the Holy and Undivided Trinity, he breathed upon it. A marvellous and wonderful thing happened. Straightway fire sent down from heaven fell upon the branch, as if the boy had breathed out flame instead of breath, and sent forth rays, vomiting fire far and wide, and dissipating the darkness all around, and so in His light he saw light and went into the House of the Lord. God, therefore, sent forth His light, and led him and brought him into the monastery, unto His holy hill and unto His tabernacles. So also he went unto the altar of God, who gladdened his youth with so clear a sign, and kindled the lamps of the Church that the Divine Office might be celebrated and performed in due season. The Lord, therefore, was his light and his salvation, that he might no longer fear any of his rivals, because He judged him and pled his cause against those unjust, envious, and deceitful boys, that their malice might no more prevail against him.

All were astonished beholding this great vision, when that torch burnt without injury to him, as once the bush which appeared to Moses was seen to burn and was not consumed. Nevertheless it was one and the same Lord who wrought the sign both in the bush and in the hazel bough ; for He who appointed Moses to be a Lawgiver to the people of the Hebrews, that he might lead them out from the Egyptian bondage, deigned to appoint Kentigern a preacher of the Christian law to many peoples among the nations, that he might rescue them from the dominion of the devil. At last that torch was extinguished, after the lamps of the church were lighted, and every one wondered more and more as they saw these great works of God. For that hazel tree from which the little branch was taken, received a blessing from S. Kentigern, and afterwards began to grow into a grove. If from that grove of hazel, as the country folk say, even the greenest twig be taken, it kindles like the driest material at the touch of fire, which as it were laps it up, and when beaten upon by but a little breath, by the merit of the Saint, it sheds from itself a fiery spray. And truly, a miracle of this kind deserved to continue, yea, to perpetuate itself in his case in whom, in the verdure of the springtime of his youth, the delight of the flesh, though outwardly flourishing, was inwardly despised, and all the glory of the world like the flower of the grass altogether withered, because the Spirit of the Lord blew upon it, and the Word of the Lord which endureth for ever, by enlightening, consecrated to Himself that most dear soul and undefiled body, and the fire of the Holy Spirit consumed him as a whole burnt offering, accepted in an odour of sweet savour.

CHAPTER VII.

Of the cook raised from the dead by the prayers of S. Kentigern.

S. SERF had a certain man deputed to the office of the kitchen, who was very necessary for him and for those who were living with him, inasmuch as he was skilled in his art and active and carefully attended to this frequent ministry. It came to pass that he was seized with a very severe illness and lay in bed; and the disease increasing and prevailing, he yielded up the breath of life. Sorrow at his death filled the heart of the old man ; and all the multitude of his disciples and all his household mourned for him, because any one equal to him in such a ministry was not easily found. Discharging the duty of nature, they consigned his native dust to the womb of all, and sustained no small loss on account of his decease. On the day after his burial, all the disciples and servants, the jealous as well as the friendly, came to the blessed Serf, earnestly beseeching him that he would by his prayer summon his Munhu, and compel him, in virtue of his obedience, so far as to endeavour to raise his cook from the dead. For those who were envious asserted that the magicians in Egypt had, by means of their enchantments, shown forth signs from heaven, and on the testimony of John in the Apocalypse, the disciples of Antichrist would send down fire from heaven, and that many wizards had in the eyes of all done what seemed wonderful things by their wicked arts, but that no one of the human race could bring back from death to the breath of life any one who was really dead, unless he were perfect in holiness.

In season and out of season they persisted, urging with persuasive words that he should prove his holiness with such a work, and that his merit would be proclaimed for ever if he recalled to life him who was dead and buried. At first the holy old man hesitated to presume to enjoin so extraordinary a work on the youth, but at length, overcome and constrained by the importunity of their wickedness, he talked to the young man of the Lord on such a matter with gentle words and prayers,

but found him reluctant, asserting that he had not merit for it.
Then S. Serf adjured him, by the holy and terrible name
of the Lord, that he should at least attempt to do what he
could in this matter, and this he commanded in virtue of holy
obedience. The young man, then, fearing that adjuration, and
deeming obedience better and more pleasing to God than all
sacrifices, went to the grave where the cook had the day before
been buried, and caused the earth wherewith he was covered to
be dug up and cast out. Then falling down upon the ground
alone, shedding many tears, and having his face covered with
them, he said : " O Lord Jesus Christ ! Who art the life and
the resurrection of Thine own who faithfully believe in Thee,
Who killest and makest alive, who bringest down to the grave
and bringest up ; to Whom life and death are servants, Who
didst raise up Lazarus when he had been dead four days, raise
again this dead man, that Thy holy name may be glorified
above all things, blessed for ever."

Then a thing exceedingly astonishing occurred.   While S.
Kentigern poured forth many prayers, the dead man, prostrate
in the dust, straightway rose again from the dead, and came
forth, though bound in grave clothes, from the sepulchral
house. He verily rose from death as the other rose from
prayer, and along with him, and a great crowd following him,
he proceeded safe and active, first, to the church to give thanks
to God, and then, by the command of Kentigern, to his accustomed office of the kitchen, every one applauding the miracle
and praising God.   But he that was raised from the dead
afterwards described the punishments of the wicked and the
joys of the righteous which he saw, and turned many from evil
to good, and strengthened in their holy purpose many who
were endeavouring to advance from good to better.   On being
urged by many he likewise unfolded the manner of his resusci-
tation.   He asserted that he was torn from things human with
unspeakable pain, and led before the tribunal of the terrible·
Judge, and that there he saw many who, on receiving their
sentence, were cast into hell, others destined to purgatorial
places, and some raised to celestial joys beyond the heavens.
And when he, tremblingly, expected his own sentence, he

heard that he was the man for whom Kentigern, beloved of the Lord, was praying ; he was ordered by a being, streaming with light, to be led back to the body and brought back to his former life and health, and he was sedulously warned by the same being who conducted him, that in future he should be watchful to live a stricter life. And the same cook, preferring sacred religion in habit and in act, and profiting, and going on from strength to strength, lived seven years longer, and then, yielding to fate, was buried in a noble sarcophagus. Likewise there was engraven on the lid of his tomb how he was raised from the dead by S. Kentigern, that by all who see or shall see it in time to come, the wonderful God may be glorified in his Saint.

CHAPTER VIII.

How S. Kentigern secretly departed from S. Serf, and what sort of miracle was wrought at his departure.

WHEN the holiness of S. Kentigern shone forth with such increasingly remarkable signs, and the fragrance of his virtues spread far and wide as the savour of life, his rivals drew unto themselves from these life-giving odours a savour of death ; and the holy reputation which furnished to many an incentive to holy conversation, fostered in them the seeds of a greater hatred towards the saint of God. The boy, prudent in the Lord, knew that the measure of their malice towards him was filled up, and that the inveterate envy that had entered into their bowels and marrow could find no rest in their unquiet hearts. Nor did he deem it safe to slumber longer beside a venomous crowd of serpents, lest, perchance, he should suffer the loss of inward sweetness. Moreover, he weighed the breath of popular fame, serenely and sweetly breathing on him and calling from every side : " Well done ! well done ! " Accordingly he resolved forthwith to leave the place, that he might in humility forsake the company of those who were hating and envying him, and prudently avoid vain glory. Upon this he took counsel, with the earnestness of the most fervent prayer, with the Angel of Good Counsel, that his good spirit might lead him in the right way, lest by any means he should run, or had run, in vain. The Lord, therefore, inclined His ear to the prayers of His servant, revealing to him by the Holy Spirit that that which he had settled in his mind would be well pleasing in the eyes of the Lord.

Therefore he secretly withdrew from the place, having God as the guide of his journey and as his protector in every place. Journeying on he came to the Friscan shore, where the river, called Mallena, overflowing its channel from the influx of the tide, took away all hope of crossing. But the good and mighty Lord, who divided the Red Sea into parts, and led Israel through the midst dry shod, under the leadership of Moses, and again turned back to its sources the perpetual flowing of the Jordan, so that the children of Israel might cross dry shod into the Land of Promise under Joshua, and who the stream of the same Jordan, at the prayer of Elijah and his disciple Elisha, divided, in order that they pass through with dry feet, He Himself now, with the same mighty hand and outstretched arm, divided the river Mallena, that Kentigern, beloved of God and men, might pass through on dry land. Then the tide flowing back in a wonderful way, and being, as I may say, afraid, the waters as well of the sea as of the river, were as walls on his right hand and on his left. He next crossed a little arm of the sea by a bridge, which is called by the inhabitants the Pons Servani, and on looking back to the bank saw the waters, which before stood as in a heap, now flowed back, and filling the channel of the Mallena, and even overflowing the afore-mentioned bridge, and entirely denying a passage to any one.

And behold S. Serf, supporting his aged limbs with a staff, having followed the fugitive, stood above the bank, and beckoning with his hand, shouted and lamented saying: "Alas! my dearest son! light of mine eyes! staff of mine old age! why dost thou desert me? Wherefore art thou leaving me! Call to mind, I beseech thee, the days that are past, and

remember the years that are gone by: how I took thee up
when thou camest forth from thy mother's womb; how I have
nourished thee, taught thee, trained thee even unto this hour.
Despise me not; neither forsake my gray hairs; but return
that shortly thou mayest close mine eyes." Kentigern, moved
by these words of the old man and melted to tears responded:
"Thou seest, O Father! that what is done is according to the
Divine Will; neither ought we, nor can we change the counsel
of the Most High; nor ought we to fail to obey His Will.
Besides there is this sea which as a great gulf is fixed between
us; so that if I would pass from hence to you I cannot, neither
can you pass from thence to me. I pray thee, therefore, have
me excused." Then the old man said: "I pray thee that by
thy prayer thou wouldest make, as thou hast just done, the
liquid again solid, divide the sea, make bare the ground, that
at least I alone may cross and come to thee on dry ground.
With willing mind will I become a son instead of a father to
thee, and a disciple instead of a teacher, that until the evening
of my days I may be thine inseparable companion." Then
again Kentigern, bedewed with tears, said: "Return, I beseech
thee, O my Father, to thine own, that in thy holy presence
they may be trained in sacred doctrine, guided by thy example
and corrected by thy discipline. The Rewarder of all reward
thee for all the benefits thou hast shown toward me, and since
thou hast fought a good fight, even now thou hast finished thy
course, and hast maintained the faith living and fruitful; henceforth there is laid up for thee a crown of righteousness, which
the Lord, the Righteous Judge, will shortly render thee. But
I, destined to the work of the ministry, will go to that to which
He Who separated me from my mother's womb and called me
by His grace, has sent me.

When these words were said, and each had given the other
his blessing, they separated, no more to look upon each other
again in this world. Serf returned to his home and awaited in
a good old age the day of his call. And thus grown old in
good days, he was gathered to the holy fathers and rested in
the Lord, and as a good labourer in the vineyard in the evening,
he received from the Lord the penny of eternal reward. And

what sort of a man and how great and in what miracles he shone, a little book written concerning his life will clearly show to those who read it. Now the place by which S. Kentigern crossed was afterwards entirely impassable. For the bridge was always after that covered with the waters of the sea, and afforded to no one any longer the means of crossing. Even the Mallena changed the force of its current from its proper place, and from that day until the present turned back into the channel of the river Ledon. So that henceforward the rivers which until then had been divided from each other, were mingled and united.

CHAPTER IX.

Of the sick man who desired and sought in prayer and obtained from the Lord that before his death he should see S. Kentigern, and tasted death in his presence, and obtained sepulture by his forethought.

THERE was a man of venerable life, Fregus by name, tormented by much and long continued sickness. The same lived in a town called Kernach (Carnoch), detained upon a bed of pain, strong in faith, wholesome in holy conversation, intent upon heaven. This man, just and full of fear, when the south wind was blowing over his garden so that the odour of its breezes reached him, felt in his heart the sweetness of the sanctity flowing from the great reputation of S. Kentigern. Whence also the desire kindling within him, both his heart and eye thirsted, so that it might have been thought that the desire which S. Simeon had to see the Lord, was renewed. For Simeon with panting spirit desired to see with the eyes of the flesh the salvation of God, the Lord's Christ clothed in flesh. Fregus, with a fixed faith, unwearied desire, and many prayers, desired of the Lord that he might see the servant of the Lord Christ, Kentigern. Christ heard the desire of both, and the ear of God hearing the preparation of their heart, fulfilled it.

Simeon's desire and joy was fulfilled to his salvation in the day
in which Christ was presented in the Temple. To his
consolation Fregus saw Kentigern the same day in which he
departed from S. Serf, and was glad. For Fregus had received
a promise from the Holy Ghost that he should not see death
until he had first seen Kentigern the Nazarite of the Lord. And
when Kentigern came to the dwelling place of the holy
sick man and knocked at the door, the sick man instructed by
a divine oracle called from within, saying: " Open the gates,
for God is with us. Come is the herald of my salvation,
promised me by God, and long waited for by me, and to-day
shown me." And when he saw him he exulted in spirit,
and giving thanks, blessed God and said : " Lord, now lettest
Thou Thy servant depart in peace according to Thy word ;
for mine eyes have seen Thy salvation which Thou hast
prepared before the face of all people, a Light for the revelation
of the True Light which lighteth every man coming into the
world and to declare the glory of eternal life to the peoples of
these and many nations." And turning to him, he again said :
" Dispose of my house and of my life to-day, and to-morrow attend to my burial, as it pleaseth thy providence, God inspiring
thee." Then by the advice of S. Kentigern, whatever of earthly
substance he possessed he dispersed and gave to the poor, and
having made a pure confession, he was anointed with the oil of
remission, and being purified with the sacraments of the life-
giving Body and Blood of the Lord, he commended his spirit into
the hands of the Lord, and with eyes and hands stretched out
to heaven expired during the words of prayer. On the morrow
Kentigern yoked two untamed oxen to a new cart on which he
placed the dead body, and having offered up prayer in the name
of the Lord, he enjoined the brute beasts to convey the burden
placed upon them to the place which God had provided for it.
And the bulls, which were not in the least restive, nor in anything disobedient to the voice of S. Kentigern, without any trip-
ping or falling and without a guide, came by a straight course,
with Kentigern and many others who were accompanying him
following, to Cathures, which is now called Glasgow, and
there with all gentleness halted with the burden of sacred earth

laid upon them (a beautiful sight) near a certain cemetery which had long before been consecrated by S. Ninian. Indeed, with no less a miracle, in no dissimilar way, and with no unequal power was this chariot by ruling and threatening directed to the aforenamed place by Him who once, when Dagon was cast down and broken, brought from Ekron to Bethshemesh, the Ark of the Covenant, which had been taken by the Philistines, placed on a new cart and drawn by milch cows which had never borne the yoke. The Saint therefore in the same place took the holy body down from the cart and having celebrated the obsequies, buried it in that cemetery, wherein was never yet man laid. This was the first burial in that place in which afterwards many bodies were buried in peace. The greatest reverence was paid to the tomb of the man of God : nor did any rash fool ever venture to trample upon or to pass over it with impunity : for within the space of a year many who trod upon it or refused to honour it were overtaken by some grievous misfortune, and some were even punished with death. That tomb is even to the present surrounded by a delicious density of overshadowing trees in token of the sanctity of him who is buried there and of the reverence due to him.

CHAPTER X.

Of two brothers, one of whom was punished by the judgment of God, the other with all his family was deemed meet to be blessed by God for many generations.

WHEN the man of God, Fregus, had been buried, S. Kentigern, as enjoined upon him by a revelation from the Lord, dwelt with two brothers who were living in the same place before his arrival, and, ordering his life in much sanctity, went on with great virtues unto perfection. One of the brothers with whom he lived was called Telleyr, the other Anguen. Anguen received God's Saint as an angel of the Lord and loved him out of the

14

most generous affection of his heart, and with all reverence and veneration obeyed his commands, submitting himself to all his injunctions. And not in vain. For the servant of the Lord blessed him in the name of the Lord. And succoured by that benediction of graciousness not only he himself but almost the whole of his posterity received a blessing from the Lord, and mercy from God our Saviour, and seemed to possess it as if by hereditary right. For He magnified them in the sight of kings and made them of great name like unto the name of the great ones who were in the earth, so that they grew and increased both in abundance of wealth, and in the culture of the Christian Religion, insomuch so that it was justly said, these are the seed which the Lord hath blessed by the prayers of his servant Kentigern.

But the other, Telleyr by name, was very troublesome to him, secretly detracting from his religion, depreciating all his actions, often openly resisting him to his face, doing him insults and injuries. Either by minishing from the good he did or by perverting it, he obscured every thing by evil interpretation. But the servant of God, who by daily custom had taught himself with blessed Job to be a brother to dragons and a companion to ostriches, and like Ezekiel to dwell with scorpions, possessed his soul in patience and was peaceful with him who hated peace. When he spoke to him of the things that belong to peace, Telleyr, perverse and ungrateful as he was, only fought against him. But God, the Lord of Vengeance, the patient Rewarder, did not finally suffer the injury done to his servant to go unavenged. For on a certain day, after many revilings by which he had embittered the soul of the just, he went forth to his work. And because he was of great strength he placed upon his shoulders a beam of great weight beyond the measure of his strength, rejoicing and thinking that he had acquired for himself the triumphal reputation of having surpassed asses in the bearing of burdens. And when he had gone a little way he tripped upon a stone and fell, and so, being crushed beneath his burden, he gave up the ghost. He learned what Solomon says: " Woe to him that is alone, for when he falleth, he hath none to lift him up." And again : " He hath fallen once for all who continually doeth evil."

Kentigern, when he heard that his adversary had fallen,
afflicted himself with great lamentations and procured for him
a place of burial ; imitating in this matter holy David the good
King of the Hebrews who mourned over the death of his
persecutor Saul and lamented him with a great lamentation.
But because, as Solomon testifies, where the fool perishes the
wise man will be more prudent, we have in the case of this man
sufficiently clear evidence that we ought to beware of offending
against the servants and friends of God, and not to dare to
inflict upon them trouble, or grievance, or injury.   For the
elect are the temple of God, and the Holy Ghost dwelleth in
them.   They are the more therefore to be deferred to, and we
should abstain from injuring them, inasmuch as He who
dwelleth in them is most powerful in vindicating their wrongs
and impartial in rendering justice to those who suffer wrong.

CHAPTER XI.

Of the election of S. Kentigern, and of his consecration as a bishop.

AND when S. Kentigern, dwelling in the above mentioned
place, became abundant in the affluence of many miraculous
gifts, it pleased Him Who had separated him from his mother's
womb, that he should no longer be hid under a bushel but
rather that he should be set upon a candlestick, that by bringing forth his righteousness as the light and his judgment as the
noonday, he might give light to all that are in the house of
God.   Therefore by Divine prompting the king and clergy of
the Cambrian region with other Christians, though they were
but very few, came together ; and after taking into consideration
what was to be done in order to restore the state of the Church
which had been well-nigh destroyed, with one consent they
came to S. Kentigern and chose him, notwithstanding his great
resistance and many objections, as the shepherd and bishop of
their souls.   He objected to their election of him, that he was
not fit on account of his youth ; but they urged the gravity of

his manners and the riches of his wisdom and knowledge. He
pled that he could not with equanimity endure the diminution
of his inward peace and holy contemplation. They alleged,
on the contrary, that it was healthful to break in on the
Sabbath of the contemplative life for the salvation of many
souls. In the end, he judged himself insufficient for this
honour, yea, rather for this burden ; but the voice of all proclaimed that his sufficiency had been declared by God with
many indications of signs and wonders. Invoking therefore
for him prosperity, and blessing him in the name of the Holy
Trinity, and committing him to the Holy Ghost, the Glorifier
and Distributor of all the orders and offices and dignities in the
Church, they enthroned him ; and having called one bishop
from Ireland, after the manner of the Britons and Scots of that
period, they caused him to be consecrated bishop. The custom
had grown up in Britain in the consecration of bishops to
anoint only their heads by pouring on them the sacred chrism,
with invocation of the Holy Ghost and benediction and the
laying on of hands ; which rite these ignorant people alleged
they had received by the institution of the Divine law and by
the tradition of the Apostles. But the sacred canons ordain
that no one shall be consecrated a bishop except by at least
three bishops, to wit, one who acts as consecrator, who shall
say over him who is to be consecrated the sacramental
benedictions and the prayers for each of the episcopal
ornaments ; and two others, who shall lay on hands along with
him, shall be witnesses, and hold the text of the Gospels
supported on his neck. Yet although the consecration to which
the Britons were accustomed, seems to be little consonant with
the sacred canons, it is nevertheless agreed that it does not
destroy the power or efficacy of the Divine mystery or of the
episcopal ministration. But because these islanders, as placed
beyond the civilized world, were, by reason of the attacks made
upon them by the pagans, ignorant of the canons, the judgment
of the Church, condescending to them, admits in that respect
their excuse. But in these times it permits no such rite as this
to be used by any one without grave censure. But S. Kentigern, though he was consecrated in this manner, took pains to

correct it in every possible way, as we shall state further on. He established his cathedral seat in a town called Glesgu, which is interpreted The Dear Family, and is now called Glasgow, where he united to himself many servants of God, a family famous and dear to God, who practised continence and lived after the manner of the primitive Church under the Apostles, with no possessions, in holy discipline, and in divine service.

The diocese of that episcopate was extended to the borders of the Cambrian kingdom, which reached from sea to sea like the rampart once built by the Emperor Severus. Afterwards by the advice and assistance of a Roman legion, in order to prevent the incursions of the Picts, a wall was built in the same place as this rampart, eight feet in breadth, and twelve in height. It stretched to the Forth, and by division separates Scotia from Anglia. This Cambrian region over which Kentigern now ruled with episcopal honour, had formerly, in the time of Pope Eleutherius, when King Lucius was reigning, received the Christian Faith, as had also the whole of Britain ; but in consequence of the pagans infesting the island and asserting their rule in it, the islanders lapsed into apostasy and cast away the faith they had received. Many had not even been washed in the saving laver. Many were tainted with the contagion of manifold heresies. Many, in name only Christians, were plunged in the slough of numerous vices ; very many had been taught by a ministry of men who were unskilled in and ignorant of the law of God. All the provincials therefore were in need of the counsel of a good pastor and the healing of a good ruler. God, therefore, the Disposer and Dispenser of all good things, provided, promoted and proposed S. Kentigern as the remedy of all their diseases, their support and their example in life.

CHAPTER XII.

How S. Kentigern conducted himself by his example and teaching in his Episcopacy; and how he bore himself both in public and in private.

THE blessed Kentigern, having taken possession of his government, as he excelled others in dignity, so he sought to exceed all in sanctity. And as he was higher in rank, so he endeavoured to appear more excellent than others in the increase of holy virtues and manners. For he thought it unworthy for him, who was bound by a Divine command to go up upon the mountain to bring good tidings to Zion, to creep on the ground and to lie at the foot. And truly it is not becoming for him who, from his office, is called to announce high things to live meanly; wherefore the Saint of God, after accepting the Episcopal dignity, always sought to exercise a greater humility and strictness than previously in food and clothing, in vigils and couches, and in the mortification of his body. And that I may briefly describe his whole life from the time of his ordination, which occurred in the twenty-fifth year of his age, down to the extreme end of his life, which lasted the space of one hundred and sixty years—breaking his fast after three and often four days, he used to revive rather than recruit his body by tasting cheap and very light foods, such as bread and milk, or cheese, or butter and some slight relish, lest his bodily frame should entirely perish after the way of this mortality; yea, that I may speak more fittingly, mortifying his members which were upon the earth by the crucifixion of a daily cross, he would by slaying offer himself for a sweet savour, a living sacrifice, acceptable unto God. From flesh and blood, from wine and from all that could inebriate he abstained altogether as one of, nay, as a chief among the Nazarites. But if at any time it happened that he was on a journey or dining with the King, he refrained from abstaining with his usual strictness. Afterwards, when he returned home, as if punishing himself for a serious crime, he increased his abstinence.

CHAPTER XIII.

Of S. Kentigern's mode of dress.

HE wore the roughest hair-cloth next to his naked body ; then a garment of leather made from the skins of goats ; next a cowl tied on like a fisherman's. Over this he was clad in a white alb, and always wore a stole placed upon his neck. He bore also a pastoral staff, not rounded, gilded and gemmed as may be seen now, but of simple wood, and merely bent. In his hand he had the Manual Book, always ready for the exercise of his ministry when necessity or reason required. And so by the whiteness of his dress he expressed the purity of his inner life and avoided vain glory.

CHAPTER XIV.

Of the couch of S. Kentigern and his vigils, and his bath in cold water.

WHAT shall I say of his bed ? I hesitate whether to call it a bed or a tomb. He lay on the rock hollowed out like a monument ; having for his head a stone in place of a pillow, like another Jacob. Verily, he was a strong wrestler against the world, the flesh, and the devil. Throwing in a few ashes, and taking off his hair-cloth, he shook off his drowsiness by destroying rather than by taking sleep. And to express myself more clearly, in a certain similitude of snatching sleep he used to bury himself with Christ. Then, when he had taken a moderate amount of sleep he rose in the night time, at the beginning of his vigils, and poured out his heart as water in the sight of the Lord his God. And thus in psalms and hymns and spiritual songs celebrating the night watches of the Lord, he exulted in the Lord and rejoiced in God our Saviour, until the second cock-crowing. Then entering into conflict with a sharper wrestling against that great and malignant dragon, which, according to the prophet, lieth in the midst of his rivers,

he was wont to strip himself of his clothes, and naked following a naked Christ, making himself naked and bare, he plunged
into the swift-flowing and cold water.   Then, verily, as the
hart thirsteth after the water brooks, so his soul thirsted after
God, the living water ; and there in cold and nakedness, with
his eyes and hands lifted towards heaven, he with devout heart
and lips chanted the whole Psalter from beginning to end.
Thereby made like one of the flock of sheep that are even
shorn which came up from the washing to Mount Gilead,
emerging from the water like a dove bathed in milk, yea, as a
Nazarite whiter than snow, brighter than milk, ruddier than
ancient ivory, fairer than a sapphire, he sat down, drying his
limbs, on a stone on the brow of a mountain called Gulath, by
the river-side, near his own hut.   And then, when his body
was dried, he put on his clothes, as if preparing his going forth
at the dawn, and showed himself as an example to his disciples.
Of this practice of bathing neither the fire of the flashing
lightning, nor hail, nor snow, nor the spirit of the storms ever
deprived him, unless a journey unavoidedly undertaken or a
very serious sickness prevented him.   But even then he was
wont to redeem the work by some other divine and spiritual
exercise.   Wherefore, by the daily use of this salutary bath,
as of a new Jordan, his flesh was restored as the flesh of a little
child ; because the law of sin which warreth in the less
honourable members was so weakened in him, and the fire of
concupiscence so mortified and extinguished, that no corruption
of the rebellious flesh, either watching or even sleeping, ever
polluted or stained the lily of his snow-white modesty.   Nor
did he feel even its simple motion either rage or stir within
him.   For through the grace of Christ working with him, his
flesh with its passions stilled, continued in the innocence of
childhood's purity.   Yea, this holy one grew up before the
Lord like an unfading lily.   And hence on one occasion he
plainly declared to his disciples that he was no more moved
at the sight or touch of the most beautiful girl than at the
sight or touch of the hardest flint.

CHAPTER XV.

Of the mode of speaking the man of God used.

IN speaking, however, he was able to control his spirit and had learned to set a watch before his mouth and to keep the door of his lips that he might direct his words with discretion. Nor did any one of his words fall lightly to the ground, nor was the word he uttered given to the winds that when found it might return unto him void. Wherefore he spoke in weight, in number, and in measure as the necessary occasion required. His speech was seasoned with salt and suited to every age and sex. Honey and milk were under his tongue and his store-house was filled with spiritual wine ; yea, even from his lips the babe in Christ sucked milk, the more advanced honey and the perfect wine, each unto his health. In judging or condemning or reproving he had not by him divers weights, nor was there respect of persons with him, but he studied the cause ; and according to the name of the fault in due time and place he administered the measure of ecclesiastical discipline with the greatest discretion. Besides, this Saint preached more by his silence than many teachers and rulers do by loud speaking. For his look, countenance, mien, gait, and the bearing of his whole body proclaimed discipline and by certain signs bursting forth like water interpreted the purity of the inner man, which lay hid there. Of his munificence which gave itself wholly to almsgiving and works of mercy, it is superfluous to commit anything to writing ; since all the substance which the Divine Bounty had conferred upon him, was the common treasury of the poor.

CHAPTER XVI.

With what grace he was deemed meet to be adorned, while he celebrated the sacred mysteries of the Mass.

BUT although in the preceding, and in similar holy exercises, he showed himself as a man, or sometimes as above man, yet

it was when celebrating the sacred mysteries of the Mass, that
he in a manner putting off the man and withdrawing himself
from earthly things, assumed something of a divine character
wholly above the human. For while with his hands raised in
the form of a cross he repeated the Sursum Corda, he lifted his
own unto the Lord, as he exhorted others. So from the golden
censer of his own purest heart filled with the live coals of
virtue, kindled with divine love, like the clearest sweet
smelling incense, his prayer, passing beyond the clouds
penetrated the heavens, and rising into the light which no man
can approach unto, was directed into the presence of God,
so that the Most High Himself vouchsafed by signs manifest
to the eyes of men to declare that He had accepted it as an
odour of a sweet savour well-pleasing to Himself. For many
times while handling the Divine Sacraments, a snow white dove
having a beak as it were of gold was seen to settle upon his
head and with the transparent fluttering of its wings to over-
shadow him and that which was laid upon the altar like a ray
of sunlight. Frequently also as he stood as a sacrificer,
sacrificing at the holy altars, a bright cloud overshadowed his
head. At times too when the Son was being immolated to
the Father, it was not he that seemed to stand there, but a fiery
pillar, by the brightness of which the sight of the beholders was
blinded. Not to all, however, was it given to know or see this
ministry, but to those only to whom it was granted by the
Father of Lights. For on one occasion when the priest of the
Lord was celebrating the Holy mysteries, a sweet smelling
cloud filled the whole house, when many were hearing the
sacred mysteries of the Lord. The odour, exceeding all per-
fumes, bathed all who had assembled themselves together in an
exceeding sweetness, and infused perfect health into many who
were there labouring with divers diseases. Verily, while I
record these things sorrow fills my heart as I see the priesthood
in the present defiled in so many ways. For while in the
meantime I am silent concerning those who simoniacally come
to sacrifice, or with Judas sell the Lord's body, since forsooth
they will not offer it except for a price, I speak of those who,
entangled in crimes and dissolute in vices, polluted in body and

soul, presume to touch and to contaminate with impure hands
the Sacrifice of Purification. Alas! in how many in the
present is the stench of foulness felt rather than the odour of
spiritual sweetness! O how more are now seized upon and
blinded by the dark whirlwind than overshadowed by the
bright cloud! Woe! woe! I say to many in the present whom
the sulphurous flame rather the surrounding pillar of fire
awaits! But now I turn back my eyes to myself and to others
like unto me, who in any way are discharging the office of the
priesthood, and for whom instead of a snow white dove at the
time of sacrifice, flies sufficiently tormenting come up from the
river of Egypt; that is, thoughts unclean, vain, unprofitable
rush into the memory from the imagination of this perishing
world. Wherefore fear and trembling come upon me, for, as
Solomon testifies, dead flies cause the ointment to stink, since
minds occupied with thoughts of this kind know little of how
great the delight is of that inward sweetness which proceeds
from the visitation of the Holy Ghost.

CHAPTER XVII.

*Of the way in which S. Kentigern withdrew himself during the whole
of Lent into more secret places in the desert and returned to his own
Church before Maundy Thursday and sometimes before Palm
Sunday.*

THE man of God persevered in the manner of life we have
described up to an extreme old age almost all the year round,
except during the days of Lent; for in those days he
was wont beyond his ordinary way to walk in a certain
newness of life. For emulating the fervour of certain holy
fathers, or rather following in the footsteps of Elijah and John
the Baptist and of the Saviour Himself, he withdrew during
every Lent into desert places, and thus separating himself by
flight from the sight of the sons of men and remaining in
solitude of body and mind, he dwelt alone; and thus more
freely devoting himself to God, away from the disturbance of

men, the contradiction of tongues and the conversation of the
world, he hid himself in the secret presence of God. Therefore
sitting alone he raised himself above himself, and often dwelling
in dens of the earth or standing at the entering in of his cave,
and praying, after the rushing of the great and strong wind and
of the fire, he heard the still small whisper of thin air breathing
upon him and shedding over him and filling him with a certain
unspeakable sweetness. Wherefore he walked about the streets
of the heavenly Jerusalem seeking for himself Him in whom
his soul delighted, and offering in his heart a sacrifice of joy,
mortifying, nevertheless, his most holy members which were
upon the earth. Presenting his most innocent body by a daily
martyrdom as an odour of sweet savour, he offered himself a
living sacrifice, holy and acceptable unto God. With what and
what sort of food he sustained his life during those days he revealed to none or at least only to a few. These, however, he
forbade with episcopal authority to disclose that mystery to
mortal man.

Nevertheless he once spake, and two of his disciples heard
the word once and simply uttered from his lips, and not
to be recalled. "I knew," he said, "a certain man, who during
Lent sustained his life on the roots of herbs only, and sometimes, the Lord granting him strength, passed the whole of
that time without the support of earthly food." Neither of
them doubted that he spake this of himself, but the man of God
suppressed his own name, in order that he might avoid vain
glory which he everywhere sought to shun. At first he used
for a long time to return home and to his disciples on Maundy
Thursday, and afterwards on the Saturday before Palm Sunday, in order to fulfil his episcopal duties, when he was received
by all as an angel of light and peace. Accordingly he was
wont to pass that week with his disciples, and on Maundy
Thursday, after the preparation of the holy chrism and oil,
washing with his own hands and tears the feet, first of the poor
and then of the leprous, and wiping them with his hair and
soothing them with many kisses,* he afterwards diligently

* Osculis demulcens, B. M.

waited upon them at table. Then for their consolation he sat at a banquet with the reconciled penitents and refreshed himself and them with bodily and with spiritual food ; and from that hour until after the celebration of the Mass on Easter Sunday he remained continually fasting. Truly on Good Friday he crucified himself with the Crucified with an incredible crucifixion, and with scourgings and in nakedness and with frequent kneeling, scarcely ever sitting down, he passed the day and the night bearing about in his own body the marks of the Lord Jesus with an exceedingly heavy cross of the soul and body.

But on holy Saturday, as if dead to the world, he buried with himself in a double tomb the true Abraham the ancient of days, and entering the sepulchre in the abundance of inward contemplation, he rested from the strifes of this stormy world, except that he appeared to celebrate the office of the day. At length, renewed in the spirit of his mind he awaited, with the sweet spices of holy virtues so diligently prepared, the most holy day of the Lord's resurrection. Then in a certain manner rising together with Christ, he feasted on the flesh of the unspotted lamb with the unleavened bread of sincerity and truth. And in the day which the Lord had made a day of joy on earth and in heaven, he rejoiced with all spiritual joy, and feasted with the brethren and a great multitude of the poor. This he was said to do at the other great festivals also. But if from any urgent cause it chanced, and it happened rarely, that he had to dine with seculars, while he slightly tasted the food set before him, he filled the guests with spiritual dainties, and, restraining the vain conversation which is wont to prevail at feasts, he concealed his own abstinence under the veil of sacred preaching.

CHAPTER XVIII.

What a bright countenance he had, and what he thought about hypocrites.

S. KENTIGERN is said to have been of middle stature, though inclining to be tall. It is asserted also that he was of robust strength, and almost unwearied in the endurance of any labour whether of body or mind. He was fair to look upon and graceful in form. Having a countenance full of grace and reverence, dovelike eyes, and cheeks like the turtle-dove, he drew towards him in love the affections of all who beheld him. And presenting the cheerfulness of his outward man as the most faithful interpreter and sign of his inward gentleness, he shed over all a certain feeling of spiritual joy and exultation with which the Lord had enriched man. For shunning hypocrisy as well in manner as in act himself, he taught all who followed him to shun it with the greatest care. And showing by examples that hypocrites are the most loathsome class of men, he instructed them with such words as these : " Beware, beloved," he said to his disciples, " of the vice of hypocrisy, which in a way is the renunciation of the Faith, the abandonment of hope, the death of charity, the cancer of chastity, the blinding of truth, the prison-house of sobriety, the fetter of righteousness, the little fox of obedience, the scant mantle of patience. And, that I may speak briefly, it is the moth of religion, the extinction of the virtues, the covert of vices, the asylum of all iniquity, the habitation of crimes. That hypocrisy is the nourisher of all evils our Lord teaches when he says that hypocrisy is the leaven of the Pharisees. For as leaven mixed with food makes it light, puffed up, and sour, so hypocrisy makes the heart of which it takes possession, void of religion, puffed up, and elated with the false praises of men, and sharp, hard and bitter against the truth of conscience, against good, against the righteous, and against those who seek after purity and holiness. And truly, beloved, while all iniquity by itself and in itself is single, hypocrisy alone in itself is double, yea, manifold. For the hypocrite, as far as in him lies, tries to blind Him who sees all things, while turning his eyes away from himself, he conceals his vices before human onlookers, under the appearance of an ostensible sanctity. And although other impious, wicked and criminal men are members of Antichrist, yet hypocrites alone are singularly and specially his followers and forerunners, as the simple followers and lovers of truth and purity are members and disciples of Jesus Christ. For Antichrist himself, as it is written, shall sit in the temple of God and by false signs show himself as if he were God. Yea, the very angel of Satan transforms himself into an angel of light ; and therefore it is not to be wondered at if his special servant and member transform himself into a servant of righteousness, since he is himself a synagogue of Satan. Believe me, for I speak to you in the truth, that the wrath of God never rages more fiercely in the Church of God than when he causeth a hypocrite to rule over it, because of the sins of the people. For also in the Apocalypse a more hurtful persecution is described as raging on the pale horse than on the rest which precede it ; because in truth the Holy Church is injured much more severely by hypocrisy, which is signified by the pale horse, than in the time of open persecutions wherein the faithful and unfaithful, the just and the unjust were made manifest and a multitude of martyrs were crowned. But clearly hypocrites by their gestures and by the bearing of their outward man make known to those who watch carefully and judge all spiritual things what kind of things lie hid within them. For while they feign the gait and bearing of the turtle-dove, contracting the shoulders, and hanging down the head, fixing the eyes upon the earth, disfiguring their faces, breathing with compressed lips, and speaking in I know not what feminine way, they by such signs make manifest their inner state. For with their gait they simulate peacocks, nay thieves ; by the contraction of their shoulders they show that they bear not in the least the easy yoke of Christ and His light burden ; by the hanging down of the head and the direction of their eyes they show that with the heart they cleave more to the dust than to the heavens, that they mind earthly things, love earthly things, and yearn with earthly desires ; but with their disfigured faces they show that they turn their backs rather than their faces to God ; and by their feminine mode of speaking, they prove that they live dissolutely and not in a manly way. To whom shall I say such are like save to jugglers, who exhibit fire, water, men, beasts, etc., in an imaginary way, where there is no reality ? But though pretenders, and cunning hypocrites, who provoke against themselves the wrath of God, may escape the opinion of those who judge according to appearance, they will in no wise deceive Him Who trieth the heart and the reins, or escape His just judgment." " These things," said the man of God, " I have said to you, beloved, not that I may make known a snare to you, or that you should not exhibit maturity of countenance, gesture, bearing, and discipline, but this I admonish you, in every way to seek God in simplicity of heart, to associate external with internal purity, and everywhere fleeing hypocrisy, to do all things with spiritual cheerfulness. Thus in all your works man shall be edified, God glorified, for God loveth a cheerful teacher and doer of good.

CHAPTER XIX.

How Kentigern converted the people over whom he was placed, and who for the most part had apostatised, to the Faith of Christ, and brought back those who had profaned the faith with unrighteous works to a more correct life.

THEREFORE the blessed Kentigern, when he had assumed the episcopacy, zealously endeavoured to discharge the duties laid upon him. And seeing that the northern enemy, that is, the prince of this world, had placed his seat in those parts and was ruling there, he took up spiritual arms to fight against him. Accordingly clad with the shield of faith, the helmet of hope, the breastplate of righteousness, and girt with the sword of the Spirit which is the word of God, he attacked the house of that strong man armed and spoiled his goods, supported by the help of the Lord of might, who is manifestly strong in battle. And to be brief, neither his foot, nor his hand, nor his tongue ceased from the completion of the journey he had undertaken, from the working of miracles, nor from the preaching of salvation, until all the ends of that land remembered and were converted unto the Lord. Those who had not yet been regenerated in the water of life, like thirsty harts, ran to the living fountain of baptism with burning desire. By this herald of salvation teaching the way of God in truth, those who had fallen away or wandered from the true faith in some erroneous doctrine of an heretical sect, when they came to themselves, and returned from the snares of the devil in which they were held captive, into the bosom of the Church, were incorporated into Christ.

Wherefore this renowned warrior began to overthrow the shrines of demons, to cast down their images, to build churches, to dedicate those which were built, to mark out parishes by fixed boundaries with the line of distribution, to ordain clergy, to dissolve incestuous and unlawful marriages, to change concubinage into lawful matrimony, to introduce as far as he could ecclesiastical rites, and to endeavour to establish whatever was consonant with the Faith, with Christian law and with righteousness. Wherever he journeyed, he was not borne on horseback, but even to an extreme old age he travelled after the manner of the Apostles on foot. When he had set all these things in order, he returned home, and betook himself to his own, and there, after his accustomed way, led a life glorious with virtues and miracles, in the perfection of the highest religion. Concerning his miracles we shall now say something which deserves to be recorded, because we do not doubt that it will be profitable to very many.

CHAPTER XX.

How S. Kentigern placed under one yoke in the plough a stag and a wolf, and how, sowing sand, he reaped wheat.

THUS, as we have said, the man of God joined to him a great number of disciples, whom he instructed in the sacred literature of the Divine Law and trained by word and example to holiness of life, and from whom he hoped to secure fellow-labourers in the harvest of the Lord. They all emulated with the emulation of God his life and doctrine, accustomed themselves to fastings and sacred vigils, were intent on psalms and prayers, and on meditation in the Divine Law, were content with sparing diet and clothing, and at certain times and seasons engaged in manual labour. For after the manner of the Primitive Church under the Apostles and their successors, they possessed nothing of their own; they lived soberly, righteously, godly, and very continently, and dwelt, as did also S. Kentigern himself, in separate huts from the time when they had become mature in age and wisdom ; and hence these "singulares clerici " were commonly called Calledei (Culdees). Thus the servant of Jesus Christ went forth to his work in the morning and sometimes to his labour till the evening, labouring chiefly in husbandry that he might not eat the bread of idleness, but rather in the sweat of his brow, both that he might set an example of industry to his disciples and have to give to him that was in need.

It happened on a certain occasion that he was altogether without oxen and that from the want of these there was no ploughing, and the land lay fallow. When the man of God saw this, he lifted up his eyes, and saw on the edge of a wood, situated close by, a herd of stags bounding along here and there through the forest. Straightway offering up a prayer, by the mighty power of his words, he summoned them to him, and in the name of the Lord, whom all dumb and unreasoning beings, animals and all the beasts of the field obey, ordered them to be yoked instead of oxen to the plough, and to plow the land. They immediately obeyed the command of the man of God, and as oxen trained and accustomed to agriculture, to the astonishment of many they ploughed the land. When unyoked from their toil, they went to their usual pastures, and at the fitting hour, like tame and domesticated, yea, like trained animals, they returned to their accustomed work. When therefore the stags had been going and returning for some time, after the manner of domestic animals, a ferocious wolf rushed upon one of them, which was wearied with labour and was cropping some food as it lay on the grassy turf, strangled it, and filled its voracious stomach with its carcass. When this came to the knowledge of the Saint, he extended his hand towards the wood, and said : " In the name of the Holy and Undivided Trinity I command that the wolf which has wrought this injury, which I have not deserved, upon me, come hither to me to make reparation." Wonderful in word, but more wonderful in deed ! At the voice of the man of God the wolf forthwith came leaping from the wood, and with a howl fell before his feet, and with such signs as it was able to make, declared that it begged forgiveness and was willing to make reparation. But the man of God upbraiding the wolf with threatening voice and look, said : " Rise ; and I command thee, by the authority of Almighty God, that thou set thyself to the plough in the place of our labourer the stag which thou hast devoured, and plough over all that remains unbroken of the little field." The wolf obeyed the word from the lips of the Saint ; and with the remaining stag yoked to the plough, ploughed up nine acres. The Saint then freely gave it permission to depart.

In this act, as it seems to me, the prophecy of Isaiah, " The wolf also shall dwell with the lamb, and the leopard shall lie down with the kid ; and the calf and the young lion and the fatling together, and a little child shall lead them," which he spiritually uttered concerning the time of our Lord's advent, was by a certain similitude fulfilled to the letter. For let the reader consider whether it is more wonderful to see a wolf lying down with a lamb or ploughing with a stag. Nevertheless, Kentigern, a most pure child, very mild in his own eyes and lowly in heart, brought this about ; yet he wrought this sign not by himself, but by the power of that Child who is born unto us, and of that Son who is given unto us. It was right that he should do this bodily who often subdued many spiritually, recalling them from wolfish cruelty and bloody slaughter, animal ferocity and a coarse life, to the yoke of faith and the plough of holy conversation.

Very many gathered together at such a sight as this, and were astonished at so unwonted a miracle. But the Saint opened his mouth and taught them, saying: "Men, brethren, why wonder ye at beholding this word? Believe me, before man became disobedient to his Maker, not only all the animals, but also all the elements, were obedient to him. But now, because of his transgression, all things are wont to be against him, for the lion to tear, the wolf to devour, the serpent to wound, water to drown, fire to burn, the air to taint, and the earth often made like iron to overwhelm with famine. And in rivalry of this wonted evil, man not only of his own accord rages against man, but man himself, by sinning against himself, also rageth against himself. But since many saints were found perfect in true innocence, in pure obedience, faith, and love, in holiness and in righteousness before the Lord, they obtained again from the Lord this power, as an ancient and natural and primordial right, and with authority commanded the beasts and elements the diseases and deaths of many."

While the holy man said many other things of this kind, those who were present were not less edified by his discourse than they were before astonished by the miracle they had seen. When the field which had been ploughed required to be sown, the Saint sought seed and found none, since all his grain had been used as food for the poor. Whereupon he betook himself to his accustomed weapons of prayer, and in faith, nothing doubting, took up sand instead of seed, and scattered it on the ground. This being done, in due season the herb grew, the seed sprouted, the blade produced the stock, and in the time of harvest brought forth the best and richest wheat, at which all who saw and heard were struck with the utmost astonishment, and his fame already great became much greater. Truly this Saint, in the power of that Grain of Wheat, which falling into the earth and dying and by rising again, brought forth much fruit, gathered corn from the sand which was sown. Moreover, he hid in the bowels of Holy Mother Church, as in the best ground, broken up by the ploughshare of the gospel, many, yea, an innumerable multitude, who were before unstable in mind and carried about by every wind of false doctrine, whose folly was heavier than the sand of the sea, and caused them, with the co-operation of God, to bring forth the corn of salvation in faith and in charity and in the performance of good works, and the Chief Householder himself deemed them worthy to be translated to the heavenly barns and fit for His own table.

CHAPTER XXI.

How St. Kentigern, assisted by Divine aid, and causing the force of the river Clyde to serve him, without any detriment transferred the barns of the King, which were full of wheat, to his own dwelling-place.

AFTER the lapse of many days, a certain tyrant, by name Morken, had ascended the throne of the Cambrian Kingdom, whom power, honour, and riches had persuaded to walk in matters which were great and strange and above him. But his heart, as, on the one hand, it was lifted up with pride, so, on the other, it was contracted and blinded by greed. The life and doctrine of the man of God he scorned and despised, slandering him in secret and sometimes withstanding him to his face, ascribing his signs to magical illusions, and esteeming all he did as nothing. But the man of God, when on a certain occasion he was in need of corn for the food of the brethren of the monastery, went to the King, and gently hinting at the poverty of himself and his disciples, desired him to come to their aid, and, according to the injunction of the Apostle, out of his abundance to supply their need. But he, elated and inflated, returned insults for prayers and threatened injuries to him who begged assistance. Then with a blasphemous mouth

he ironically said to him : "Cast thy care upon the Lord and
He will sustain thee, as thou hast often advised others, for
there is no want to them that fear Him, but they that seek the
Lord shall not want any good thing.   Thou, therefore, though
thou fearest God and keepest His commandments, art in need
of everything, even of thy necessary food.   But I, who seek
not the kingdom of God nor His righteousness—to me are
added all good things, and plenty of every kind smiles upon
me."   Finally he said: "Thy faith therefore is vain, and thy
preaching false."

But the holy man, arguing on the other side, proved from
the testimonies of the Holy Scriptures and from the instruc-
tive declarations of reason, and by examples, that many just
and holy men were in many ways in this life afflicted with
thirst and want, and that reprobates were exalted by opulence,
affluence of delights, and the highest honours.   And when
with power and clearness he taught that the poor would be the
patrons of the rich by whose benefits they are sustained, and
that the rich need the support and protection of the poor as
the vine that of the elm, the barbarian was unable to resist his
wisdom and the Spirit who spoke through him, but angrily
responded : "What more dost thou desire ?   If, trusting in thy
God, thou canst without human hand transfer to thy house all
my corn which is contained in my barns which thou seest, I
willingly yield and bestow it upon thee, and for the rest I will
be devoutly obedient to your demands."

As he said this he retired joyfully, as one who by such an
answer had mocked the holy man.   But when the evening was
come, the Saint, with his eyes and hands raised to heaven and
weeping profusely, prayed very devoutly to the Lord.   In the
very hour when from the inmost depths of the Saint's soul
tears rose up and flowed from his eyes, the river Clyde, which
flowed beneath him, by the will of Him who has power in
heaven and on earth, in the sea and in all deep places, suddenly
came down and became swollen, and overpassing its banks
flowed round the barns which stood there, and licking them up
drew them into its channel, and swiftly transported them to dry
land at a place called Mellingdenor, where the Saint was at

that time in the habit of residing. Then the river at once
ceased from its fury, and broke down within itself its swelling
waves, because the Lord placed gates and bars that they should
not advance further nor pass beyond their appointed bounds.
These barns were found there whole and uninjured, and not
only not a sheaf, but not even a blade appeared to have been
wetted. Lo! in this, though in a different element, we see the
sign repeated which we read of as having already been wrought
in the Chaldaean furnace, into which the three children, free in
their religion, but otherwise bound, were cast. For as there the
fire had power to burn only their bonds, not their bodies or
their clothes, so here, water was able to transpose the barns
filled with corn, but not to wet them. When the multitude
had seen that in the name of the Lord His servant had wrought
so great a sign, they said: "Truly great is the Lord, and
greatly to be praised, who has thus caused His Saint to be
magnified."

CHAPTER XXII.

*How the aforesaid King Morken, at the instigation of his military
follower Cathen, struck S. Kentigern with his foot, and with what
punishment both of them were visited.*

AFTER the current of the river had, by thus carrying across
the fruits of the earth, made glad the city of God, in which
those who had been enrolled as fellow citizens of the Saints
and of the household of God were assembled together to serve
the living God, that faithful and wise servant, made steward in
the house of the Great Householder, distributed the measure
of wheat to each of his fellow servants, dividing to every one
according to his need. What was over he dispersed abroad
and gave to the poor; nor did he send any needy one who
begged empty away. But the aforesaid King Morken, though
very rich and great in the eyes of men, yet being a vile slave
of Mammon, bore ill the loss, as it seemed to him, of his stock

of corn, and from the sign which had happened to him by the
will of heaven, whence he ought to have had joy and gladness
to his own advantage, he took scandal to his soul. Just as the
solar ray is pleasant and delightful to healthy eyes and lends
its aid to their sight, yet ministers the material of darkness to
the diseased and to those under the influence of hemlock ; therefore his eye being consumed because of his fury, he belched
forth many reproaches against the holy bishop, calling him a
magician and a sorcerer. And he commanded that if ever he
appeared again in his presence, he should suffer the heaviest
penalties as one who had ridiculed him. For a certain very
wicked man who was the King's confidential friend, Cathen
by name, had urged him on to hatred and injury of the bishop,
because the life of the good is wont to be hateful and burdensome to the wicked, and the mind inclined to evil readily yields
to one who persuades it to that which it embraces. For an
impious leader, according to Scripture, has all his servants
wicked, and very often chooses such for his counsellors, as
pour venomous whispers into ears which willingly listen to
unjust things, and diligently blow up the fire of malice with
the breath of accusations, adding fuel to make the flame burn
higher, so that it does not die away of itself, but rages the more
fiercely. But the man of God, wishing to extinguish malice by
wisdom, approached the presence of the Prince in the spirit of
meekness rather than with the rod of severity ; and, instructing and warning him after the manner of a most gentle father,
sought to correct the folly of a son. For he knew that by the
melodies of the sweetly sounding harp of David the madness
of Saul had been allayed, and that, according to the sentence
of Solomon, the King's wrath is appeased by patience. But
the man of Belial, like the deaf adder that stoppeth her ears
lest she should hear the voice of the charmer, charm he never
so wisely, yielded not to the warning word, the counsel of
safety. Nay, excited by fiercer madness, he rushed upon him,
struck him with his heel, and smote him to the ground upon
his back. But the Saint, that his doctrine might be known by
his patience among the bystanders, bore most patiently the
hurt and the ignominy, committed his cause to the vindication

of the Supreme Judge, and so departed from the presence of this sacrilegious King, rejoicing that he was deemed worthy to suffer reproach for the word of the Lord. Cathen, the instigator of this sacrilege, mounted his horse, laughing loudly, and departed full of joy, as one who seemed to himself to have triumphed over the Saint. But behold judgment went forth from the face of the Lord to do justice on behalf of his servant who had suffered injury. He had not gone far from the crowd assembled in the place when the prancing steed on which he sat, struck its foot on I know not what stumbling-block, fell down, and its rider, falling backwards before the gate of his lord, broke the neck which he had raised so proudly against the Lord's bishop, and expired. Also a swelling attacked the feet of the King, pain followed the swelling, and death the pain. He died in the royal town, which is called after his name, Thorp-Morken, and was buried. Nevertheless, the disease was not cut off or buried in the succession of his family. For, from the beginning of that time forward, the weakness ceased not, gout became hereditary in his family, and his descendants take after him, though not in look or habit of body, yet in this kind of disease. For the fact that this royal race has become extinct through this kind of disease, proclaims by the witness of death how the Lord, who is zealous for His own and the avenger of such, visits the sins of the fathers upon the children for many generations, and how great the retribution is which he inflicts upon the proud. After this the Saint dwelt for many days in great quietude in his city of Glasgow and in his own diocese, and had peace in the circuit thereof, because the divine vengeance which had been shown forth upon his persecutors, ministered to others motives of fear, reverence, love, and obedience towards the Saint of God, and afforded him the opportunity of doing whatever he wished according to the will of God.

CHAPTER XXIII.

How S. Kentigern, avoiding the snares of those who lay in wait for his death, departed from the borders of his own country, and went to S. David, who was dwelling in Wales.

AFTER some time had elapsed, certain sons of Belial, a generation of vipers, of the kindred of the above-named King Morken, incited by the sting of intense hatred, and infected with the poison of the devil, took counsel together to take Kentigern by craft, and to put him to death. But, fearing the people, they did not dare to go about that evil deed openly, because all held him as their teacher, and as the bishop and shepherd of their souls, and loved him as an angel of light and peace. Frequently they laid many snares for him in order that they might suddenly shoot their arrows against him, but the Lord became unto him a strong tower, that his enemies, the children of iniquity, might not prevail against him. At last they bound themselves by a strong oath not to cease until they had accomplished the wicked compact in which they had conspired against his life, nor through fear of any one to fail in one unjust or treacherous word they had resolved upon against him. When the man of God learned this, although he might have repelled force with force, he thought it better for a time to leave the place and give place to wrath, and to seek elsewhere a richer harvest of souls, rather than to bear about with him a conscience seared as with a hot iron, or even darkened on account of the death of any man, however wicked. For the blessed Paul, the chosen vessel, gave him an example of acting in the same way, when at Damascus he saw a death without fruit hanging over him, and sought the basket and rope to escape and avoid it, and yet afterwards at Rome joyfully submitted to it with great gain.

At length, taught by divine revelation, he departed from those regions, and journeyed towards Wales, where at that time the holy bishop David was shining forth in his episcopal work like the star of the morning, when, with its rosy face, it brings in the day. Wheresoever the Saint went, virtue went

forth of him to the healing of very many.   And when he had
come to Carlisle he heard that many in the mountains were
given to idolatry or were ignorant of the Divine Law.
Thither he turned, and God helping him and confirming the
word with signs following, he converted to the Christian religion many who were alien from the faith and others who had
erred in the faith.   O, how beautiful upon these mountains
were the feet of him that brought good tidings, that published
peace, that brought good tidings of good, that published
salvation, that saith unto Zion, Thy God reigneth.   He
tarried some time in a certain thickly crowded place to con-
firm and strengthen in the faith the men who were dwelling
there, where he also erected a cross as the sign of their salvation, from which the place received in English the name of
Crosfeld, that is, Crucis Novale.   In this same locality a
basilica, which has recently been built, is dedicated to the
name of the Blessed Kentigern ; and in order that he might
show forth his sanctity, he is not doubted to have shone forth
in many miracles.

Departing from this place, the Saint next directed his steps
along the sea-shore, and scattering the seed of the Divine
Word wherever he journeyed, he gathered a great and fruitful
harvest in the Lord.   At length he reached S. David, safe and
sound, and found in him greater works than fame reported.
But the holy bishop David rejoiced with exceeding joy at the
arrival of such and so great a guest.   With eyes overflowing
with tears, and with many mutual embraces, he received
Kentigern as an angel of the Lord, dear to God, and retaining
him with him for some time, he always honoured him to a
wonderful extent.   These two sons of light, therefore, dwelt
together, attending upon the Lord of the whole earth, as two
lamps shining before the Lord, whose tongues became the
keys of heaven, that by them a multitude of men might be
deemed meet to enter therein.   These Saints were joined
opposite to each other as the two cherubims in the Holy of
Holies in the temple of the Lord, having their faces bent down
towards the mercy-seat.   In frequent contemplation of
heavenly things they stretched out their wings on high ; in

the ordering and dispensing of earthly things they folded them down. They touched each other mutually with their wings, while, by the instruction of each other in the doctrine of salvation, and in the alternate exercise of virtues, they excited each other to the more earnest perfecting of holiness. Thus these Saints, whether beside themselves unto God, or whether sober for our cause, they have left to posterity an example of laying hold on and attaining to eternal life.

When S. Kentigern had abode there for some time, the fame of him spread through the mouths and ears of very many, and led him to the acquaintance, familiarity, and friendship of many, not only of the poor and middle class and nobility of that land, but also of King Cathwallain, who governed the country. And the King, knowing him to be a holy and righteous man, heard him willingly, and after hearing him did many things which pertained to the salvation of his soul. And when the King on several occasions asked him the reasons why he had left his own country, and he had made them known to him, and said that he wished to have the power of building a monastery in which he might unite a people acceptable to God, and zealous of good works, the King replied : " My land is before thee ; wherever it suits thee and it seems good in thine eyes, construct the habitation of thy dwelling-place and build a monastery. Yet, as it seems to me that the place which is called Nautcharvan is more suitable than all others, inasmuch as it abounds in everything necessary, I assign it to thee." The man of God gave frequent thanks to the King, and chose for his building and habitation that place which had even already been marked out for him by a divine intimation. Therefore, blessing the King, he departed, and bidding farewell to S. David, each bestowing upon the other his benediction, he betook himself to the aforesaid place with a great multitude of disciples, who had flocked around him, preferring to lead a life of poverty with him in a strange land rather than to live luxuriously without him in their own.

CHAPTER XXIV.

How S. Kentigern, following a wild boar, found a suitable place.

THUS the most holy Kentigern, separated from S. David in bodily presence but by no means absent from his love, and from the vision and observation of the inward man, gave no sound sleep to his eyes, nor quiet rest to his eyelids, until he found a place fit for building a tabernacle to the Lord God of Jacob. Therefore, with a great crowd of disciples with him, he went round the land, and walked through it, exploring the situations of the places, the quality of the air, the richness of the soil, and the sufficiency of the meadows, and pastures, and woods, and the other matters which pertain to suitability for the erection of a monastery. And while they proceeded together over steep mountains, hollow valleys, and caves of the earth, through thickets of briers, dark woods, and open glades in the forests, they talked together as they went of the things which pertained to the matter they had in hand, when lo! a solitary wild boar from the wood, entirely white, met them, and approaching the feet of the Saint, moving its head, sometimes advancing a little, and then standing still and looking back, motioned to the Saint and his companions with such gesture as it could that they should follow it. On seeing this they marvelled and glorified God, who works things marvellous and past finding out in His creatures, and followed step by step their leader, the boar, which went before them.

When they came to the place which the Lord had predestinated for them, the boar stood still, and frequently striking the ground with its foot, and making the gesture of tearing up with its long tusk the soil of the little hill that was there, by shaking its head again and again and grunting, it showed clearly to all that that was the place designed and prepared for them by God. The place is situated on the bank of the river which is called Elgu, from which to this day, as it is said, the district takes its name. Then the Saint, on bended knees, giving thanks adored the Almighty Lord, and rising from prayer, he blessed the place and its surroundings in the name of the Lord ; and then, in testimony, and as the sign of salvation and as an earnest of future religion, he there erected a cross and pitched his tents. The boar, however, seeing what was done, approached with frequent grunts as if about to request something from the bishop. But the Saint, scratching the head of the beast, and stroking his mouth and teeth, said : " God Almighty, in whose power are all beasts of the forests —the oxen, the fowls of the air, and the fish of the sea—grant thee such reward for thy conduct as He knoweth is best for thee." Then the boar, as if well remunerated, bowed its head to the priest of the Lord, departed, and sought again its well-known woods.

On the following night, when the man of God, yearning after divine things, lifted up his hands in the sanctuary and blessed the Lord, it was revealed to him from on high that he should dwell in that place, and that he should there construct a monastery in which the sons of God, who were scattered abroad, might be gathered into one, so that coming from the east and from the west, and from the north and from the south, they might be deemed meet to sit down with Abraham, Isaac, and Jacob in the kingdom of heaven, and that God Himself would provide for them, and be the protector of the place and of them that dwelt therein. With what truth this revelation was sustained, the issue of events by its manifest fulfilment showed. For at the dawn of day he made known to others the oracle which had been divinely shown to him, and cheered on the souls of those who heard him to set about the building. For, like bees making honey, they did not slumber in ease, but all in the sweat of their brow laboured strenuously at the work. Some cleared and levelled the ground; others, when the ground was levelled, laid the foundations. Some felling trees, others carrying them, others fitting them together, they began, as the father had marked out for them by measurement, to build a church and the other offices of planed wood, after the manner of the Britons, for of stone they were not yet able to build, nor was it then the custom.

While they were pressing on the work, and the building was growing under their hands, there came a certain heathen prince,

Melconde Galganu by name, with his soldiers, and a great multitude with them. A fierce man and ignorant of God, in the indignation of his wrath he demanded who and whence they were, and how they had dared to presume to do such things upon his land. To his questions the Saint humbly replied, that they were Christians from the northern parts of Britain, and were come thither to serve the living and true God. He asserted that he had begun to build the house there by the permission, yea, rather through the kindness, of King Cathwalain, his master, in whose possession he believed the place lay. But he, furious and raging, ordered them all to be driven away from the place, and whatever they had built to be pulled down and scattered, and then began to return to his own house. Thus the man departed, breathing out threaten-ings against the servants of Christ, and lo! the chastening hand of the Lord touched him, and smote him with a sudden blindness. Nevertheless, as was clear in the end, this happened to him not for foolishness to himself; for, while he sat in the utter darkness, the true morning star shone into his heart, and when the outward light was for a time taken away, drew him out of the darkness and shadow of death and led him with the light of truth. Wherefore inwardly enlightened and induced by penitence, he caused himself to be conveyed by his servants to the man of God, whom he began to entreat devoutly to dispel the blindness by his prayers, and wash him in the font of salvation.

Then the Saint who studied not to be overcome by evil, but to overcome evil with good, desired to render to the man good for evil. For having offered up prayer, he laid his healing hand upon the blinded man in the name of the Lord, and signing him with the cross of salvation, both turned his night into day, and again, after darkness, poured into him the light he hoped for and eagerly desired. Thus the Lord smote that He might heal, and making the new Paul out of the old Saul, He blinded that He might give light. Immediately, therefore, on receiving his sight, he was washed by the holy bishop in the saving water, and thenceforward he was an active and devoted fellow-worker in all that he desired of him. Taking an account of all things in his possession, he bestowed them with royal munificence on S. Kentigern for the construction of his monastery, and, aided by his assistance, he speedily brought the work he had begun to completion.   In the church of the monastery he established the Cathedral Chair of his bishopric, the diocese of which was the greater part of the adjacent country, which by his preaching he won for the Lord. In truth, he led back to the way of salvation a countless num-ber who were either ignorant of the Christian faith or averse from it, or had been depraved by profane teaching, or debased by wicked works ; and, by his labours, made vessels of wrath vessels of mercy, and vessels of dishonour vessels of glory. For he went forth from his monastery to perform the episcopal office, travelling through his diocese as time permitted.   But, as he never found where the foot of his desire might long rest, as the dove to the ark from the face of the deluge of the world, so he returned to the beloved quiet of his monastery.   Yet he bore with him the olive branch with its green leaves, because he received the fruit of the peace and mercy he preached to others.

CHAPTER XXV.

With what number of brethren the monastery flourished, and how the holy boy Asaph carried fire without being burnt.

THERE flocked to the monastery of the man of God old and young, rich and poor, to take upon them the easy yoke and the light burden of the Lord.   Nobles and men of the middle class brought their children to the Saint to be brought up in the nurture of the Lord.   The multitude of those who renounced the world increased from day to day both in number and quality, so that the number of those who enlisted in the army of God amounted to nine hundred and sixty-five, who professed in act and manner the monastic rule according to the institu-tion of the holy man.   He divided this company, which had

been gathered and devoted to the divine service, into a
threefold division for the observances of religion. To three
hundred, who were illiterate, he assigned the duty of till-
ing the ground, herding the cattle, and other necessary labours
outside the monastery. Another three hundred he appointed
to duties within the walls of the monastery, such as preparing
food and building the offices. The remaining three hundred
and sixty, who were lettered, he appointed to celebrate the
divine services in the church day and night ; nor did he readily
allow any of them to cross the threshold from the holy places,
but directed them to remain together within as if in the sanctuary of the Lord. Those whom he found to be more
advanced in holiness and wisdom, and apt for the teaching of
others, he was accustomed to take with him when, from
necessity demanding or reason requiring, it behoved him to go
forth for the discharge of his episcopal duties. But, dividing
into bands and choirs those whom he had set free for the
divine service, he ordained that when one choir finished the
service of God in the church, another immediately entering
should begin it, and when that had finished, another should
thereupon enter to celebrate. Thus the sacred choirs being
conveniently and discreetly arranged, and following each other
in turns, while he performed the work of God continually,
prayer was regularly made to God without ceasing by the
Church there, and by praising the Lord at every time, the
praise of God was continually resounding in their mouth.
Truly, glorious things were said in and of that City of God,
for in it was the habitation of all who were joyful, so might
fittingly be said of it that prophecy of Balaam : " How goodly
are thy tents, O Jacob ! and thy tabernacles, O Israel. As the
valleys are they spread forth as gardens by the river's side."

There flourished in that glorious monastery men holy and
perfect, shining wrestlers, like Jacob, against the world, the
flesh, and the devil. By faith, love, contemplation, yearning
intently after the vision of God, like true Israelites, fruitful in
good works, humble in their own eyes, and therefore as well-
wooded valleys fragrant with holy thought and bathed in
rivers of Scripture, and thus also, like the cedars beside the

16

waters, glorious in all those many virtues and signs. Among them was one Asaph by name, distinguished by birth and presence, shining in virtues and miracles from the flower of his earliest youth. He sought to follow the life and teaching of his master, as may be learnt more fully by reading a little book of his Life, from which I have thought fit to insert in this work one miracle, because the perfection of the disciple is the glory of the master. For on one occasion, in the time of winter, when the frost had contracted and congealed everything, S. Kentigern, having according to his custom recited the Psalter naked in the coldest water, and having after putting on his clothes gone out in public, he began to be greatly oppressed by the intensity of the cold, and in a manner to become entirely rigid, so that it was clearly given to be understood what was of himself and what was of the power of the divine condescension. For, since when naked in the water, he endured for so long a space the icy cold without being frozen, it is clear that in the frail vessel of his human body divine virtue operated, and in the fact that he became rigid, though clad in skins and other garments, human fraility is recognised. The holy father therefore ordered the boy Asaph to bring fire to him, at which he might warm himself. The Lord's child ran to the oven and begged that coals might be given to him. And when he had nothing in which to carry the burning coals, the servant said to him either in joke or seriously: " If thou wish to take the coals, spread out thy dress, for I have nothing at hand in which thou mayest carry them." The holy boy, fervent in faith, and trusting in the sanctity of the master, without hesitating, having gathered up his dress, held it out, and received into his lap the live coals, and carrying them to the old man cast them forth in his sight from his bosom, without any sign of burning or corruption being apparent on his dress. The greatest astonishment, therefore, took hold upon all who were present because the fire carried in the dress had not in the least burnt combustible material. A friendly dispute arose between the father and his holy disciple concerning this sign, for the one seemed to maintain his ground by assertions to which the other as justly objected. The bishop

ascribed the working of the sign to the innocence and obedience of the holy boy ; the boy asserted that it was done on
account of the merits and sanctity of the bishop, obeying whose
command and trusting in whose holiness he had ventured to
attempt it. And indeed, without prejudice, I think that this
miracle is more correctly to be attributed to the merits of
each wise one, inasmuch as each of them had always from
his earliest years preserved the members of his body, which are
the garment of the soul, white in virgin chastity, and because
the oil of divine charity was never wanting from the head of
either. The dress of the disciple suffered neither hurt nor
injury from the fire in order that the integrity of both might
be rightly made manifest. For if the fire of unchaste love
had been hid in their bosoms, their clothes, according to the
words of Solomon, would have been burnt. And if their garments had been rolled in blood, that is, if the members of their
bodies had been stained with the pollution of prurient lust from
the will of the flesh or of blood, doubtless, according to Isaiah,
it would have been the presage of burning and the fuel of fire.
S. Kentigern, therefore, who up to this time had held the
venerable boy Asaph dear and beloved, from that day henceforward regarded him as the dearest and best loved of all, and
as soon as he conveniently could, raised him to holy orders.
In due season, moreover, he delegated to him the care of the
monastery, and made him his successor in the episcopate, as
we shall hereafter relate.

CHAPTER XXVI.

*How he saw S. David crowned in heaven by the Lord, and what he
predicted concerning Britain.*

ON a certain occasion, while the man of God continued longer
and more intently in prayer than was usual with him, his face
seemed as if glowing with fire, so that the bystanders were
filled with amazement and ecstasy. They beheld his counten-

ance as the countenance of an angel standing among them, and
as they saw his face shining as the face of another Moses,
wonder and amazement took hold upon them all. When his
prayer was finished, he withdrew apart and sat down and gave
himself up to the most vehement grief. His disciples, knowing that his grief would not be without great cause, drew near
to him with fear and trembling, and humbly besought him, if
it were permissible and not displeasing to his paternity, to
reveal to them the cause of such great grief. The Saint was
silent for a little, but as they perseveringly knocked at the ears
of that most pious father, he at length gave way, and responded in these words : " Be it known to you, my dearest sons,
that the most holy David, the honour of Britain, the father of
his country, the most precious carbuncle of prelates, has just
left the prison of the flesh, and rich in merits has been introduced among the splendours of the saints, and penetrated into
the Holy of Holies. I say unto you, believe me, that not only
has a multitude of holy angels, flooded with light, conducted
him as he entered with heavenly music into the joy of the
Lord, but the Lord Jesus Christ Himself, meek and lowly in
heart, went forth, as I saw, to meet him at the gates of Paradise, and crowned him with glory and honour. Behold, like a
matchless light to his generation, and a most brilliant star
which shone by word and example, he has become present to
him who under his charge calls upon him that he may shine
with delight for Him who made him, and assist all who ask his
protection, seek his help, and celebrate his sacred memory.
And truly, dearest ones, it behoves me to rejoice in the glory
of such a father, who loved us beyond others, but the ardent
affection of devoted love permits me not to abstain from tears.
Know that the world of Britain, deprived of such a light, of a
patron so devoted, and of one so powerful before God and with
all the people, will feel the absence of him, who ever placed
himself between that region and the sword of the Lord, half-
drawn on account of the wickedness of those who dwell therein,
lest when entirely drawn it should smite even to destruction.
The Lord will surely deliver Britain up to strange nations who
know not God, pagans in religion, and the island will be

emptied of its original inhabitants, and the religion of the
Christian law there is in it will be scattered until the appointed
time ; but again, by the mercy of God, the Ruler of all things,
Christianity shall be restored to its former state, yea to a
better." These things the Saint said and was silent; fear
seized upon all who heard him, and the shower of their tears
poured forth.   But desiring to be further informed on this
matter, they quickly sent a messenger to the church over which
S. David presided as bishop, and they found that the Saint of
God had passed away from this world in that same hour in
which the man of the Lord, instructed by a divine oracle, had
announced it to them.   In this matter it must be considered
how great was the merit of that man in the sight of God, who
beholding not with the eye of flesh but by the vision of the
heart, was deemed meet to see such glory, and delivered so true
a prophecy concerning the Britons and the Angles, which all
England was able, by a faith which sees, to verify.

CHAPTER XXVII.

*How S. Kentigern went seven times to Rome and consulted the blessed
Gregory concerning his orders.*

THE blessed Kentigern, knowing that Britain was smitten in
in many provinces by the Gentiles, and that the Church
of God .established therein was in many ways perverted
from the faith of Christ by idolaters, and divided ; discovering, moreover, that it was frequently assailed by
heretics, and that there were many things contrary to sound
doctrine and alien from the integrity of the faith of our Holy
Mother, the Catholic Church, deliberated within himself for a
long time what remedy he could apply for all these evils.   He
resolved at last to visit the seat of S. Peter, which was
founded on a rock, and that the tares might not grow up
among the wheat, he endeavoured by means of the sound
teaching of the Holy Roman Church, and through the know-

ledge of the articles of the faith, to cast away from his mind
every scruple of doubt, so that he might arrive by careful
investigation at the light of the truth. For Britain, during the
reign of the most holy King Lucius, had received, under the
papacy of Eleutherius, the faith of Christ through the preaching of the most excellent teachers, Faganus and Divianus, and
others, whom Gildas the Wise, the historian of the Britains,
commemorates ; and the Christianity thus received, it preserved
whole and undefiled down to the time of the Emperor Diocle-
tian. Then the moon was turned into blood, and the flame of
persecution against the Christians burnt brightly through the
whole world. Then that scourge inundated Britain and
vehemently oppressed it, and a pagan hand mowing the first-
fruits of that island, namely Alban, took him out of the midst
thereof to be recorded in the Book of the Eternal King ; and
shortly after innumerable others, voluntarily and in ignorance,
it also offered up to heaven.

From that time the worship of the idols began to spread in
the island, and brought in rejection and forgetfulness of the
Divine Law. Nevertheless, after this Christianity in some way
revived and flourished. But in process of time, first the
Pelagian heresy springing up, and then the Arian creeping in,
defiled the face of the Catholic Faith. Yet it renewed itself,
and again grew when these heresies were cut down and cast out
by S. Germanus, Bishop of Auxerre, a man truly Apostolic,
and made illustrious by many signs ; but the invasion of the
neighbouring Picts and Scots, hostile to the recognition of the
name of Christ, entirely drove away the faith and the faithful
from the northern parts of Britain.

Afterwards, Britain was conquered by the Angles, who were
at that time pagans, after whom it was called Anglia. By
them the natives were driven out, and the land was made
subject to idols and idolatry. The natives of the island, however, fled beyond the sea into Little Britain or into Wales, and
though driven from their own country they did not all
altogether abandon their faith. But the Picts, first chiefly
through S. Ninian, and afterwards through S. Kentigern and
S. Columba, received the faith. Then relapsing into apostasy,

through the preaching of S. Kentigern not only the Picts but also the Scots and innumerable people settled in divers parts of Britain, were again, as we have already said, and as we shall say more at length, either converted or confirmed in the faith.

S. Augustine, however, noted for his monastic life and habit, and other religious servants of God, who were sent by the Supreme Pontiff, the blessed Gregory, came to Anglia, and being rich in showers of preaching and glittering with the lightning of miracles, either by themselves or by means of their disciples, converted the whole island to Christ, instructed them fully in the rules of the faith and in the institutes of the Holy Fathers, and filled the whole land of Anglia with the sweet savour of Christ.

Because therefore Britain had been crushed by so many misfortunes, and because Christianity had so often been obscured or even destroyed in it, there had arisen in it at divers times divers rules contrary to the form of the Holy Roman Church and the decrees of the Holy Fathers. In order, therefore, that he might learn and be able to meet and remedy all these, the blessed Kentigern left the above-mentioned monastery, visited Rome seven times, and brought home what he there learned was needed for the correction of Britain. But as he returned the seventh time to his fatherland, a most grievous malady seized him, and he reached home with the greatest difficulty.

On one occasion he visited Rome when the blessed Gregory was presiding in the Apostolic seat, a man apostolic by office, authority, doctrine, life, and the special Apostle of Anglia, for the Angles are the signs of his Apostleship. As a vessel of solid gold adorned with all manner of precious stones, he was rightly called the Golden Mouth, for when expounding he elucidated many parts of Scripture by his clear and highly polished style. His memory is as the work of the apothecary in making up an unguent, and as music at a banquet of wine. For by his mellifluous writings and the hymns which he composed according to the laws of music, he gladdened, and by his canonical institutions he strengthened and adorned the House of God, the Holy Church scattered throughout the world.   To this most holy Chief Pontiff he laid bare his whole life, and set before him in order his election to the episcopacy and consecration, and all things that had happened to him. But the holy Pope, strong in the spirit of counsel and discretion, as filled with the Holy Ghost, and knowing him to be a man of God and full of the grace of the Holy Ghost confirmed his election and consecration, because he knew that both had come from God.   And on the bishop on many occasions seeking it, and with difficulty obtaining it, he supplied the things which were wanting to his consecration, and set him apart to the work of the ministry which had been laid upon him by the Holy Ghost.   The holy bishop Kentigern having received the Apostolic absolution and benediction, returned home, bringing with him precepts, codes of the canons, and many other books of Holy Scripture, as well as privileges and many relics of the saints, ornaments of the Church, and other things which belong to the adornment of the House of God.   And he gladdened his own by his return, both by religious gifts and blessings.   He dwelt there for some time in great peace and [holy] conversation, and ruled holily and firmly both his see and his monastery with great care.

CHAPTER XXVIII.

What he knew, by revelation of the Spirit, of two clerics, and what happened to them according to his prediction.

IT came to pass that the holy president had to confer sacred orders by ordaining clergy and promoting some to the priestly office.   Among others, there was brought to him for promotion to the priesthood, a certain cleric of elegant appearance, great eloquence, and much learning, a Briton by birth, but educated among the Gauls.   When the Saint saw him, he summoned the archdeacon, and ordered him to be immediately removed and separated from the clergy. For to the eyes of the Saint, as it were, a sulphurous flame seemed to proceed from the bosom of this cleric, and to assail his nostrils with an unbearable stench. By this vision, revealed to him by the Holy Spirit, he was made aware of the vice which reigned in his body. For he was, as was then made known to the man of God alone, but afterwards to all others, addicted to that most foul crime for which the Divine vengeance overthrew and destroyed with fire and brimstone the sons of unbelief in the Five Cities. And the Saint said to those around him: "If the sacred canons forbid women on account of the infirmity of their sex, which is no wise in blame, to be promoted to the rank of the priesthood, much more are we bound to banish from a rank and office so sacred men who are perverters of their own sex, abusers of nature, who, in contempt of the Creator, in degradation of themselves, in injury of all creatures, cast off that in which they are created and born, and become as women. Nowhere do we read of a heavier penalty being decreed than against that monstrous race of men among whom that execrable crime was first conceived. Not only did it overthrow those cities with their inhabitants with fire, on acccunt of the burning of libidinous passion, and with brimstone because of the stench of that abominable sin, but it also turned them into a lake horrid to the sight, full of brimstone and bitumen, and intolerable stench, receiving nothing living into itself, having indeed on its shores trees that produce fruits outwardly sound, but inwardly full of smoke and ashes, and presenting an image of the punishments of hell. And this indeed shows distinctly enough how horrible so dreadful a pleasure is, and how it ought to be avoided by all in this life, and with what torments it will be visited in the future ; while the fire expresses the heat of the passion, the brimstone the stench of the crime, the bitumen the bondage of the vice, the smoke the blindness of heart in this world, and in the world to come the unquenchable fire, the intolerable stench, the indissoluble chains, the horror of darkness, everlasting death." After this the aforesaid cleric went his own way, and, as fame has noised abroad, died, cut off by a sudden death.

But when the holy man had finished the office, and was returning, there met him, among others, a cleric, a most eloquent foreigner. Beholding him the man of God gazed at him with burning eye and asked who he was, whence he came, and for what purpose he had come into those parts. He replied that he was a preacher of the truth, teaching the way of God in truth, and asserted that he had come into those parts for the salvation of souls. But when the Saint had conversed with him, he convicted him of being intoxicated with the poison of the Pelagian pestilence. Willing, therefore, that he should return rather than perish, he earnestly warned and reasoned with him to renounce the pernicious sect, but found his heart stony as to conversion. Then the Saint ordered him to be expelled from his diocese, and denounced him as a son of death, and that the death of body and soul was in his gates. He remembered also the saying of the Apostle : " A man that is a heretic after the second admonition, reject ; knowing that he that is such is subverted." The same son of hell departed, expelled from those borders, and attempting to cross a certain river, was choked in the water and descended into hell ; and thus, by an evident proof, showed the exceeding trustworthiness of the veracious prophecy of the most holy man.

CHAPTER XXIX.

How the Divine vengeance smote the adversaries of S. Kentigern, and bore down upon his countrymen who had apostatised.

HITHERTO we have related, as carefully as we could, what S. Kentigern did when he withdrew from his own country and dwelt in a foreign land. Let us now turn back and show point by point what his adversaries suffered, how he returned to the Cambrian region, and what he did there. When the man of God, yielding to malice, departed, his enemies were not long suffered to rejoice over his departure. For the Lord visited them with a heavy hand and a strong arm, and with fury poured out, holding over them a rod that was vigilant for evil and not for good, smiting them with the blow of an enemy and with cruel chastisement, even to destruction. For some, darkness obscured, the gloom of blindness following; others paralysis enervated, enfeebling all their strength, and rendering them effete as to their bodily powers. Some an incurable madness seized, and retained its hold upon them even to the grave; others a contagious leprosy devoured or struck down, making them, as they breathed in their half-dead bodies, like unto the putrescent dead. Many of them became epileptic, and exhibited a dreadful spectacle to those who saw them. Some in one way and some in another were consumed by various kinds of incurable diseases, and died. So great was the indignation of the wrath of God, and so suddenly did He destroy them, that all who knew their power and numbers before, hissed over at them, saying : " Wherefore hath the Lord done thus to this people? since lo! they have suddenly come to an end and perished on account of the iniquity which they wrought against the holy one of the Lord, striving to take away from the earth his life and memory."

Even his countrymen quickly abandoned the way of the Lord, which the good shepherd and true teacher had shown them ; and, as dogs returned to their vomit, had relapsed into the rites of idolatry. But not with impunity. For the heavens and the earth, the sea and all that is therein, withdrew from them their obedience, use, and wonted aid, so that, according to the Scripture, the whole world seemed to fight against these foolish ones, and the elements were thought unable to bear with equanimity the absence of so great a man when banished from that land. For, according to that prophecy, "All men departed, all the cattle died, the heaven above was as brass, the earth as iron, devouring the inhabitants thereof, and a consuming famine prevailed for a long time over all the earth."

But when the time came for having mercy, that the Lord might remove from them the rod of his indignation, and that they might be converted to the Lord, and that He should heal them, He raised up over the Cambrian kingdom a King Rederech by name, a most Christian King, who had been baptized into the faith in Ireland by the disciples of S. Patrick, and who sought the Lord with his whole heart, and endeavoured to restore Christianity. And truly it is a great sign of the Divine pity when the Lord ordains for the government of the holy Church and for the dominion of the earth, rulers and kings who judge righteously and live holily, who seek the good of their people, who execute judgment and justice in the earth. So, moreover, on the other hand, it is an evident proof of the wrath of God when He causes a hypocrite to reign because of the sins of a people, when He calls the King apostate and the rulers unjust, as it is written in the book of Job, and when, according to the prophet, He gives kings in his wrath and princes in his anger.

CHAPTER XXX.

How holy Rederech invited S. Kentigern by messengers and letters to return to his own see in Glasgow, and how the holy prelate, taught by a divine oracle, acquiesced in the petition of the King.

KING REDERECH, therefore, seeing that the Christian religion was almost entirely destroyed in his kingdom, anxiously considered how he might restore it. And after deliberating about it for a long time in his own mind, and with other Christians who were in his confidence, he found no plan by which it would more surely be brought about than to send messengers to S. Kentigern to recall him to his first see. The fame of the Saint going forth smote on the ears and mind of the King, for his light could not be hid, although it was shining in regions more remote. The King, therefore, despatched his messengers to the holy prelate with letters deprecating his refusal, warning, praying, exhorting, and adjuring him by the name of God as a shepherd no longer to withdraw his care from the sheep of his pasture, long desolate and destitute, by longer absence, lest he should expose them to be carried off and torn to pieces by the open mouth of the infernal wolf ; but rather to hasten to them before they were altogether swallowed by the throat

of the roaring lion seeking whom he might devour, since none
but he can deliver them, and there is none more justly bound
to do so.   He declared that it was wrong for the spouse to
desert his bride, the shepherd his flock, the prelate his church,
for the love of whom he ought to lay down his life, so that he
might not be a hireling.   He intimated also that those who
had sought his life had died by the vengeance of God, and he
swore that in all things, as a son his father, he would obey his
will, his teaching, his commands.

When the holy father received this he was silent, nor did he
on that day return any definite answer.   For he had proposed
to nourish his grey hairs to the evening of his life, and to end
his days in that glorious monastery which he had built with
long and great labour ; to lay himself down to sleep in peace,
and to take his rest in the sight of them, his sons, whom he
had begotten in the Gospel and brought forth in Christ.   But
because he sought not his own, but the things which are of
Jesus Christ, and came not to do his own will but the will of
Him that sent him, and desiring it to be done concerning himself in himself and towards himself, as it would be in heaven,
he submitted himself entirely to the Divine disposition.   And
when, on the following night, he prostrated himself in prayer
and consulted the Lord on the matter, the angel of the Lord
stood beside him, and a light shone in the part of the oratory
in which he was, and the angel smote him on the side and
commanded him to arise.   And when he stood up the
heavenly messenger said to him : " Return to Glasgow to thy
church, and there thou shalt be for a great nation, and the
Lord will make thee to increase among his people.   Thou
shalt acquire for the Lord thy God a holy nation, an innumerable people to be won unto the Lord thy God, and from Him
thou shalt receive an everlasting crown.   For there thou shalt
end thy days in a good old age, and shalt pass from this world
to thy Father who is in heaven.   Thy flesh shall rest there in
hope, buried with glory and honour, much honoured by the
frequent visits of the peoples, and by the exhibition of miracles,
until, in the last day, by receiving a double robe at the hand
of the Lord, thou possessest a double reward in the general

resurrection." These words being said, the angelic vision and address ceased. But he, weeping copiously, gave thanks to the Lord, frequently groaning : " My heart is ready, O God ; my heart is ready for whatsoever may be pleasing to Thee."

CHAPTER XXXI.

How the Saint, addressing his disciples concerning his return, appointed S. Asaph as his successor in the government.

WHEN the day dawned, he assembled his disciples together, and said unto them : " I speak as a man to you, dearly beloved, I wished, after long yearning and deliberation, according to the infirmity of my flesh, these, mine aged eyes, to be closed by you, and my bones to be hidden in the womb of the mother of all in the sight of all of you. But since it is not in man to direct his steps, it has been enjoined upon me by the Lord to return to mine own church of Glasgow ; nor ought we, nor dare we, nor will we contradict the words of the Holy One, as Job saith, or in any wise go against it, but rather in all things obey His will and command, even to the end of life. You, therefore, dearly beloved, stand fast in the faith ; quit you like men, be strong, and seek always to do all your things in charity.' These and many similar things he said in their presence, and lifting up his hand he blessed them all. Then, with the unanimous consent of all, he appointed the aforesaid S. Asaph to the government of the monastery, and by petition of the people, and by canonical election of the clergy, successor of his bishopric, and again delivered a profound and lengthy sermon concerning faith and hope and charity, on mercy and justice, humility and obedience, on holy peace and mutual patience, on avoiding vice and acquiring virtue, on observing the institutes of the Holy Roman Church, on the regular discipline and exercises which he had established to be observed with all diligence, and on constancy and perseverance unto the end in all good things.

When the sermon was ended he enthroned S. Asaph in the cathedral seat, and again blessing and bidding them all farewell, he went forth by the North door of the Church, because he was going forth to combat the Northern enemy. When he had gone out that door was closed, and all who saw or heard of his going out or departure bewailed his absence with great lamentations. Hence the custom grew up in that church that that door should not be opened except once a year, on the festival of S. Asaph, that is, on the kalends of May, for two reasons. First, in deference to the sanctity of him who had gone forth ; secondly, because thereby was indicated the great grief of those who had bewailed his departure. Therefore, on the day of S. Asaph that door is opened, because when he succeeded the blessed Kentigern in the government their mourning was turned into joy. From that monastery a great part of the brethren, to the number of 665, being in no wise able or willing, so long as he lived, to live without him, went with him. Only three hundred remained with S. Asaph. With such troops, as if compassed about by the host of the heavenly court, he returned to fight the old enemy, and from the ends of the North, in which the apostate angel had placed his seat, to drive him out. And truly those who accompanied him were counted by such a number, who multiplying the senary exercise of good works by fulfilling the decalogue of the Law, arrived at the centenary perfection of virtues, and maintained the quinary guard over the discipline of the senses so far as they were able.

When King Rederech and his people heard that Kentigern had come from Wallia into Cambria, from exile into his own country, the King with great joy, and a great multitude of people rejoicing and praising God, went out to meet him. On account of his arrival there sounds in the mouth of all thanksgiving and the voice of praise and gladness, while in the mouth of the holy prelate there resounded glory to God in the highest, peace on earth, and good will towards men.

CHAPTER XXXII.

Of the devils miraculously driven away, and of the place where he stood to preach, and of the fertility of the land which ensued.

BLESSED Kentigern, when he saw the concourse and approach of a great multitude hastening towards him, rejoiced in spirit, gave thanks to God, and knelt down in prayer. When he had finished praying he rose up, and, in the name of the Holy Trinity, blessed the assembled multitude. Then, as if fortifying those who stood around him with the sign of the Holy Cross, he addressed them as follows : " Whoever envy the salvation of men and oppose the word of God, I command them, by virtue of that same word of God, that they forthwith depart and present no obstacle to them that would believe." Whereupon, with exceeding speed, a vast multitude of phantoms, horrible in stature and appearance, issued out of that crowd and fled away in the sight of all, and great fear fell upon all who saw them. The holy champion, comforting and strengthening them, laid bare the natures of those in whom they had believed, and encouraged the hearts of all who stood around him to believe in the living God. For by clear reason he showed that idols are dumb, vain inventions of men, fitter for the fire than for worship. He showed, likewise, that the elements in which they believed as gods are creatures and formations adapted by the disposition of their Maker to the use, service, and help of men. But Woden, whom they, and especially the Angles, had believed to be their principal God, from whom they derived their origin, to whom they had consecrated the fourth day, he affirmed, with probability, had been a mortal man and King of the Saxons, by faith a pagan, from whom they and many nations had derived their descent. His body, he said, many years having passed, was turned into dust, and his soul, buried in hell, endures the eternal fire.

By these and similar arguments he cast out the worship of idols from their hearts, and proved to them the Almighty God, Three and One, to be the Creator of all things, from the very beauty of the visible creation ; and afterwards preaching to them the faith that is in Christ Jesus and the Sacraments of the Faith, he showed by the most true and lucid demonstrations that there is none other name under heaven whereby believing men may be saved, save the name of our Lord·Jesus Christ. And when, by the instruction and dictation of the Spirit, he had taught many things in this way which pertain to the Christian Faith, in the flat field which is called Hoddam, the ground on which he sat grew, in the sight of all, into a high hill, and remains there even to this day. Therefore those who had come together, beholding so sudden and so great a miracle, obeyed the word of faith in their inmost hearts, and believed firmly and faithfully that Jesus Christ is God, who had revealed Himself to them by His servant Kentigern. All eagerly therefore, both men and women, old men and young, rich and poor, as one man, flocked to the man of God and were instructed in the rules of the faith. After being catechised, they renounced Satan and all his pomps and works, and were washed in the saving laver in the name of the Holy Trinity ; and so, anointed with the sacred chrism and oil, were incorporated into the body of the Church and made members of Christ.

The Bishop, therefore, rejoiced with great joy in that a great salvation had been wrought, and great happiness increased among the people ; nor was there less joy in the presence of the angels of God in heaven, because so great a multitude had been converted unto God. Appropriately by such a sign as the elevation of the mountain at the beginning of his preaching did the Lord will to magnify His saint, who, by that same preaching, did effectually bring all to believe as unto that same mountain, compacted and fruitful, in which God was well pleased to dwell. That Stone first cut from the mountain without hands grew into a great mountain, and filled the face of the whole earth, for the Omnipotent God, born of the Virgin, without human passion, clearly shone forth throughout the breadth of this world. Christ, I say, is that Mountain exalted on the top of the mountains, even the Lord Himself, who surpasses all the power and greatness of all the saints, in whose ways, paths, and light, by the instruction of Kentigern, these natives walked much more devoutly and consistently than that carnal house of Jacob, who, loving darkness rather than light, and going back from the ways of the truth, have scorned to be enlightened by the Supreme Light.

But after the inhabitants of Cambria had turned to God and were washed in the laver of salvation, all the elements which seemed to have conspired together for their ruin, to avenge the wrong done to God, now put on a new face towards them for the salvation both of their bodies and their souls. For as the Lord turned away from the apostates and opposed them by forbidding even the dew to fall, and commanded the clouds not to rain upon the earth, and summoned a devastating famine upon them, so when He turned to those who had returned to Him, He commanded the heaven to yield rain, and the earth to bring forth green herb, and to produce its fruits for those who dwelt thereon.   Thus, by the Lord causing His face to shine upon them, the sun was seen to be brighter than usual, the vault of heaven clearer, the air more wholesome, the earth more fruitful, the sea calmer, the abundance of all things greater, peace surer, the aspect of all things more joyful, and therefore the devotion of all in the observance of Divine worship was more profuse.

CHAPTER XXXIII.

How King Rederech conceded to him power over himself and his posterity.

KING REDERECH, therefore, seeing that the good hand of God was with him, and was working according to his desires, was filled with great joy, and made no delay in openly showing with what great devotion he was animated.   For, stripping himself of his royal robes, he, on bended knees and joined hands, with the consent and advice of his lords, did homage to S. Kentigern, and handed over to him the dominicn and princedom over all his kingdom, and desired him to be the King, and himself to be appointed the ruler of the country under him, in like manner as he knew the great Emperor Constantine had formerly done to S. Silvester. Hence the custom arose that, during the course of many years, so long as the Cambrian kingdom lasted in its own right, the Prince was always subject to the Bishop. Frequently was this saying inculcated by the King that not in vain, but rather of set purpose, had he been called Kentigern by S. Servanus, because, by the will of God, he ought to become the head lord of all, for " Ken " is " caput " in Latin, and the Albanic " tyern " is interpreted " dominus " in Latin.

S. Kentigern made, as it were, a new Melchizedeck, did not hesitate to receive what the King so devoutly offered to the honour of God, because he foresaw that in the future even this would be to the advantage of the Church of God. Moreover, he had the privilege sent to him by the Supreme Pontiff that he should be subject to no bishop, but should rather be styled and should actually be the Vicar and Chaplain of the Pope. But the King, who exalted the holy bishop with glory and honour, received grace for grace, and greater honours and riches from the Lord. Likewise his Queen, Languneth by name, bowed down by the opprobium of long continued barrenness, by the blessing and intercession of the holy bishop, conceived and bare a son, to the consolation and joy of their whole kindred. The Saint baptized him and named him Constantine in commemoration of the act which his father had done to him in resemblance of that which the Roman Emperor had done, as we have already said, to S. Silvester. He grew up a boy of good disposition, in stature and grace, beloved of God and men, and by hereditary right, when his father yielded to fate, he succeeded him in the kingdom, but was always subject to the Bishop, even as his father before him. And because the Lord was with him he overcame all the neighbouring barbaric nations without bloodshed. All the Kings who ruled in the kingdom of Cambria before him he surpassed in riches, glory, and dignity, and, what is better, in holiness. Whence also famed for his merits, and finishing his course in peace, he was deemed worthy to triumph over his age, and to be crowned

with glory and honour in heaven, and even to the present day
he is wont to be called by many S. Constantine. We have
said this as it were by anticipation, because we have made
mention of Constantine as begotten by the prayers of S. Kentigern, and baptized and educated by him. The holy prelate
Kentigern built churches and ordained priests and clerics in
Hodelm, and fixed his see there, for a certain reason, for some
time. Afterwards, warned by a Divine revelation, justice demanding it, he transferred his seat to his own city of Glasgow.

CHAPTER XXXIV.

*How many nations the Saint, now by himself, now by means of his
disciples, cleansed from the foulness of idolatry, and how he was
distinguished by many miracles.*

BLESSED Kentigern, like a burning torch, in his days endeavoured, by the radiant flames of his virtues and the burning
and shining word of God, to enlighten the hearts blinded by
the error of ignorance, to kindle in the cold the love of God,
to burn up the thorns of sins and the tares of vices which,
because of the ancient curse, had grown up upon the face of
the earth and covered it. Nor was there any one who could
easily hide himself from his heat. For he carefully visited his
diocese, removed all strange gods from the midst of them, and
cast forth all ceremonies of foreign worship. And so preparing
the way for the Lord, and making the paths of our God
straight, he restored the whole of Christianity there to a better
state than it had been in before.

Then the soldier of God, consumed with the fire of the
Holy Spirit, like a fire which burns the wood, and as a flame
setting on fire the mountains, after he had corrected that which
was nearest to himself, namely, his diocese, went forth to more
distant places, and cleansed from the foulness of idolatry and
the contagion of heretical doctrine the land of the Picts, which
is now called Galwiethia, with the adjacent parts; and with

shining miracles, brought back to the rule of truth whatever
he found contrary to the Christian Faith and sound doctrine,
and amended it as far as lay in his power. In all these things
the fervour of his devotion was not turned aside, but his hand
was stretched out still to greater works and to the increase of
the glory and honour of the name of the Most High, his feet
having been shod with the preparation of the Gospel of Peace.

For he went to Albania, and there with great and well-nigh
intolerable labour, often exposed to death by the snares of the
barbarians, but standing in the faith undeterred, the Lord
working with him and giving power to the voice of his preaching, he converted that country from the worship of idols and
profane rites, which are almost equal to idolatry, to the ways
of faith, to the customs of the Church and to canonical institutions. For there he built many churches, dedicated them
when built, ordained priests and clerics, and consecrated many
of his disciples bishops. Moreover, in those parts he founded
many monasteries, and placed fathers over them from the
disciples whom he had instructed.

In all these things his spirit, yearning for the salvation of
the many, did not rest unless as a glorious standard-bearer of
the Lord of Hosts, and a wrestler of unconquered mind, he
were fighting the battle of the Lord. Therefore he sent forth
those of his own whom he knew to be strong in faith, fervent in
charity, eminent for doctrine, and lofty in religion, to the isles
which are afar off, towards the Orkneys, Norway, and Iceland,
to proclaim among them the name of the Lord and the faith
of Jesus Christ, because in those places the harvest was indeed
great, but there were no labourers. And since he was now old
and unable to go to them himself, he desired that this work
should be accomplished by his disciples.

These things being duly performed, he returned to his own
Church in Glasgow, where, as also elsewhere, yea everywhere,
he is known to have shone with many and great miracles. For
wheresoever his lips disseminated the knowledge of salvation,
the virtue of God working in His servant manifested its
efficacy by manifold signs. For to the blind he gave sight, to
the deaf hearing, to the lame the power of walking, to the

dumb speech, to the insane reason. He drove away fevers,
cast out devils from the bodies possessed, gave strength to the
paralytic, healed lunatics, cleansed the lepers, cured all manner
of diseases. But in works of this kind was his daily employ-
ment, his accustomed play, his assiduous custom, which in a
manner became common from so frequent occurrence, and
which, lest their number should beget weariness, have not here
at least been written down. Frequently, also, many sick were
taken to the bishop to be healed by the touch of the hem of
his garments, often by mouthfuls of food or drink given or
received ; also men, borne on a bed, were healed by the shadow
of his body as he passed by, so that he might have been
thought another Peter.

CHAPTER XXXV.

*How the Lord preserved the clothes of the Saint untouched by any
particle of rain, snow, and hail.*

ALTHOUGH the hand of the Lord wrought by blessed Kentigern many miracles not commonly vouchsaved to other saints,
He wrought one particular work in him at which all men
wondered. For as all bare witness who knew the man, as well
as those who conversed with him, never during his lifetime
were his clothes wetted with showers of rain, or with snow, or
with hail pouring down and falling upon the earth. For often
standing in the open air, while the inclemency of the weather
increased, the rain pouring down like bilge-water and flowing
in different directions, and the spirit of the storm raging
around him, he from time to time stood immovable, or went
where he would, and yet always remained uninjured and untouched by any drop of rain from any quarter. And not on
him alone did the Lord vouchsafe to work this prodigy, which
was the Lord's doing, and wonderful in the eyes of all, but
also the whole crowd of his disciples who were going along
with him, by his merits oftentimes, though not as in his own

case always, experienced the same grace on themselves and for themselves. For the sanctity of the holy teacher Kentigern, who was bedewed with Divine grace, was for his followers a shadow in the daytime from the heat and a refuge from the wind and rain.

Let no one, therefore, disbelieve that the Lord bestowed the blessing of the miracle we have described upon his most devoted servant, to the praise of his name and in commendation of his holiness, since in a mannér similar to this, yea in a manner greater than this, He vouchsaved in the desert to confer a boon upon the whole of the Hebrew people to show the favour which they had found in His sight. The garments of that people, as we read, were not worn away, nor grew old ; the garments of this man alone were never wetted with drops of rain from heaven. Therefore, to none let this seem incredible, for, as the Lord says, all things are possible to him that believeth, and with God nothing is impossible. Likewise, also, the sign which in the smiting of Egypt, as in a certain place we find written concerning the children of Israel, we know was frequently repeated in the case of blessed Kentigern. For when darkness covered the whole land of Egypt, and thick darkness the people, as it is written, where the children of Israel dwelt there was light ; so, often, when a cloud covered the whole land, bringing a darkness that might be felt, where the Saint was preaching, around himself and the place, and all the inhabitants thereof, light shone. Rightly, therefore, as we believe, never wet with rain were the garments of this Saint, who endeavoured with all care to preserve the members of his body clean and untouched by any defilement of flesh and blood. With justice also did a light shine forth upon the darkness around him in the place of his preaching while he taught the people ; in his heart the Sun of Righteousness, the True Light that knows no setting, ever shone, and he himself, like a lamp in a dark place, gave light in the midst of a wicked and perverse generation, according to the word of the Apostle Peter.

CHAPTER XXXVI.

How the Saint miraculously restored to the Queen a ring which she had
improperly given away, and which had been thrown by the King
himself into the river Clyde.

S. KENTIGERN, therefore, having returned home, as we have
said, intending to live alone in mental solitude, apart from the
throngs of men, willed not to be readily seen in public or to
go abroad except in case of great urgency, yet he ceased not,
though against his will, to shine forth in wondrous signs.
Queen Langueth, whom we mentioned above, rich in wealth
and pleasures, was not faithful, as she ought to have been or as
it became her, to the royal chamber or marital bed, for the
abundance of her treasures, the superfluity of her luxuries, and
the pride of power, were wont to minister incentives and fuel
to the will of the flesh.   She cast her eyes upon a certain
youth, a soldier, who, after the perishable beauty of this
perishing flesh, seemed to her fair to look upon and of great
beauty beyond many who were with him at Court.   And, as
one who of himself is ready for such service without incitement
from another, he was easily induced to sin with her.

And when the days passed, and the unlawful pleasure,
frequently repeated, had become more and more pleasing to
both, for bread eaten in secret and stolen waters, according to
Solomon, seemed to be sweeter to them, so from a rash act
they were overmastered by a blind love.   And a royal ring,
set with a precious gem, which her lawful husband had in-
trusted to her as a special mark of his conjugal love, she
imprudently and impudently gave to her paramour.   But he
more impudently accepted the ring and placed it on his finger,
and by such a sign opened the door of suspicion to all who
were acquainted with the matter.   A faithful servant of the
King discovering the secret of the Queen and soldier, took
care to instil it into the King's ears.   But the King did not
easily lend his ear or mind to him who told him of his disgrace
and the unworthiness of his wife.   An old and true proverb is:
" It is difficult for a cuckold to put faith in one who reveals

the failings of a beloved wife ; and he is more apt to turn his hatred back upon the accuser than against the accused." But the informer of the adultery, in proof of the matter, showed the ring on the finger of the soldier, and by this persuaded the King to believe him, and kindled in him the spirit of jealousy more fiercely.

The King, therefore, being assured of this secret, veiled under a calm demeanour the wrath of his soul against the Queen and the soldier, and bore himself towards them with more than his wonted cheerfulness and familiarity. But when a day more serene than usual occurred, he went to hunt, and summoning the soldier to accompany him, he sought the woods and the forests with a multitude of hunters and dogs. The dogs being uncoupled, and the hunters being scattered in divers places, the King came down alone with the soldier to the banks of the river Clyde, where, in a shady place and on the green turf, they each thought it would be pleasant to sleep a little. The soldier, worn out with fatigue, and suspecting no danger, reclining his head, stretching out his arms, and opening his hand, straightway slept ; but the spirit of jealousy exciting the King, who feigned to be sleeping, did not suffer him either to sleep or rest. Accordingly, seeing the ring on the finger of the sleeper, his eye was blinded with madness, and he could scarcely keep his hand from his sword and refrain from shedding his blood. Nevertheless he controlled his rage, and drawing the ring from the sleeper's finger, threw it into the neighbouring river, and then rousing him up, ordered him to join his companions and return home. The soldier awoke from sleep thinking nothing of the ring, and obeyed the King's command, and never noticed what he had lost until he entered his house.

But when, on the return of the King, the Queen went forth from her chamber to salute him as usual, she received from the mouth of him she saluted, invectives, threats, and continual reproaches, and with flashing eyes and menacing countenance he demanded where the ring was which he had entrusted to her keeping. She replied that she had it deposited in a casket. The King, in the presence of all his courtiers, commanded her to bring it to him with all haste. She, still full of hope, entered into the inner chamber as if to seek the ring, but straightway sent off a messenger to the soldier telling him of the enraged King's demand, and bidding him send the ring with all haste. The soldier sent back word to the Queen that he had lost the ring, and could not tell where he had lost it ; and, fearing the face of the King, he took refuge in concealment, and absented himself from the Court. Meanwhile, as she sought further delay, and was slow in producing what she was of course unable to find, vainly seeking an empty nothing, the King, incensed with rage, and frequently calling her an adulteress, broke into curses, saying: "God do so to me and more also if I do not judge thee according to the law of adulteresses, and if I do not condemn thee to a most disgraceful death. Thou, clinging to a young adulterer, hast neglected the King, thy husband, yet I had made thee the sharer of my bed and the mistress of my kingdom. Thou hast acted in secret ; I will act openly, and in the sight of the sun I will make manifest thy ignominy, and reveal thy most shameful deeds before thy face."

And when he had said many things of this kind, all his courtiers prayed for some delay, and he with difficulty conceded three days, but ordered her to be imprisoned. Cast into a dungeon, she was already anticipating the death which, as it were, was hanging over her, but none the less did her guilty conscience torment her. O heavy and intolerable punishment, the damning testimony of a guilty conscience! Although one condemned to punishment may have outward peace, yet is he acknowledged to be wretched and disturbed whom a gnawing conscience ceaselessly persecutes. The spirit, therefore, of the guilty woman was vexed within her, and with a lowly and contrite heart, and with tearful prayers, she implored God that He would not enter into judgment with His handmaiden, but that according to His great mercy, as He formerly had pity on the woman taken in adultery and placed in the midst before Him, He would design to pity her in the same case. By the inspiration of the Lord, therefore, the woman in her great strait found out a wise devise. Sending a trusty messenger to S. Kentigern, she told him all her misfortune, and from him, as her only deliverer, earnestly desired help. She also begged that he would at least use his influence with the King and beseech pardon for her, because there was nothing so great that he would or could or ought to deny him.

The holy bishop, instructed by the Holy Spirit and with virtue from on high, and acquainted with the whole story in order before the messenger arrived, ordered him to go with a hook to the banks of the aforesaid river Clyde, and to cast the hook into the stream, and to bring back to him immediately the first fish that was caught with it and taken out of the water. The messenger did what the Saint told him, and exhibited in the presence of the man of God a large fish which he had caught, and which is commonly called a salmon. He ordered the fish to be cut open and gutted, when there was found in it the aforesaid ring, which he immediately sent by the messenger to the Queen. When she saw and received it, her heart was filled with joy, her mouth with exultation and thanksgiving; her mourning was turned into joy, the expectation of death into the dance of exultation and safety. The Queen therefore rushed into the midst, and before the eyes of all, restored to the King the ring he had demanded back.

The King, therefore, and all his Court with him, were sorry for the injuries intended against the Queen, and humbly on his knees he sought her forgiveness, and swore that he would inflict a very heavy punishment, even death or exile, if she willed it, upon those who had informed against her. But she, wisely understanding that pity rather than the award of judgment was what she had to do with, was desirous that he should shew mercy, as it becomes a servant always to do to a fellow-servant. "Far be it, my lord, O King," she said, "that any one should suffer anything of the kind on account of me ; but if thou desirest that from my heart I should forgive, what thou hast done towards me, I desire that thou wouldst put away all angry feeling from thy heart, as I do, against my accuser." And all, when they heard this, wondered and were glad. And so the King and Queen and the accuser were recalled into the grace of peace and mutual love with each other. The Queen,

as soon as she could, went to the man of God and confessed
her guilt to him, and making satisfaction by his advice, carefully corrected her life for the future, and kept her feet from a
similar fall.   Nevertheless the sign by which the Lord magnified His mercy towards her she never made known to any one
during her husband's lifetime, but after his death she told it to
all who wished to know it.

   Behold the Lord, sitting in heaven, repeated by His saint,
Kentigern, what He deigned to do while He was clothed in
the flesh and dwelt upon the earth.   Peter, casting a hook into
the sea, at His command drew out the first fish which came, in
the mouth of which he found the piece of money, which he
gave in tribute for the Lord and for himself.   So by the command of S. Kentigern, in the name of the Lord Jesus Christ,
the Queen's messenger casting a hook into the river, took a
fish, and bringing it to the Saint, found in it when brought
and opened a ring with which he saved the Queen from a
double death.   In both cases, as it seems to me, there was
rendered unto Caesar the things which are Caesar's, and to
God the things which are God's.   For in the piece of money
there was returned to Caesar his image, and in the ring restored
to the flesh, the flesh was redeemed from destruction, and the
soul made in the image of God was washed from sin and
restored to God.

CHAPTER XXXVII.

*How a Jester, despising the King's gifts, demanded a dishful of fresh
   mulberries after Christmas, and how he received them through the
   instrumentality of S. Kentigern.*

KING REDERECH was magnified by the Lord because he
clung to Him, by serving Him in faith and good works, and
by obeying the will of S. Kentigern.   For glory and riches
were in his house, generosity was in his heart, urbanity in his
mouth, and munificence in his hand, because the Lord had

blessed the work of his hands. Hence not only within the confines of his own country was the fame of his liberality spread, but also beyond the sea in Ireland. Wherefore a jester from one of the Kings of Ireland, who was skilled and clever in his art, was sent to Cambria to the court of the aforesaid King, that he might see whether the truth responded to his fame so far and widely spread. Admitted to the court, the jester played with his hand on the tympanum and cithera, and rejoiced the King and his paladins all the days of the festivity of Christmas. When the feast of the Lord's holy Epiphany was ended, the King commanded gifts to be brought forth and bestowed upon the jester as became his royal munificence. The jester refused them all, asserting that he could have enough of such things in his own country. Being asked by the King what he would be willing to accept, he replied that he had no need at all of gold or silver, vestments or horses, in which Ireland abounded. "But if thou desirest," he said, "that I should leave thee well remunerated, let there be given to me a dish full of fresh mulberries." Those who heard this speech proceed from the mouth of the man burst into laughter, because they thought he was joking and speaking playfully. For a servant of this kind is wont to be more highly esteemed in proportion as excites to laughter and to words that move to mirth. But he, with an oath, declared that he had demanded the mulberries in all seriousness and not as a joke ; nor could he in any way be moved from his purpose either by prayers, promises, or the offer of the most ample gifts, and rising, he intimated that he wished to retire from the midst and to carry off, as the saying is, the King's honour. But the King took this very ill, and inquired of his companions what could be done in the matter that he might not be dishonoured. For it was then winter, and not a mulberry could be found anywhere. Therefore, acting on the advice of his courtiers, he went to S. Kentigern, and humbly begged that by prayer he would obtain from God what was demanded. The man of God, although he thought that his prayer would not be fitly offered for such trifles, yet because he knew that the King had a great devotion to God and to Holy Church, and recognised his imperfection in this matter, the holy prelate resolved to condescend to his petition, since he hoped that by such means he might be able to advance him in virtue. Therefore, deliberating with himself for a little, and praying briefly, he said to the King: "Rememberest thou in what place during the summer thou didst cast away the garment in which thou wast girded because of the great heat, when thou wast hunting, that thou mightest follow the hounds more quickly, and then forgetting or slighting it, thou didst not return to take up what thou hadst cast off?" The King replied: "I know, O Lord, my King and bishop, the time and the place." "Go," said the Saint, "quickly to the place, and thou shalt find the garment still whole spread out over a bush of thorns, and beneath it mulberries sufficiently ripened, still fresh and fit for gathering. Take them and satisfy the demand of the jester, and in all things concern thyself that thou more and more honour God, who will not allow thy honour to be harmed or diminished in so slight a thing." The King did as the bishop directed him, and found all as he predicted. Taking a dish, therefore, and filling it with the mulberries, he gave it to the actor, saying: "See, take that which thou askest for; for by the hand of the Lord working with us, thou canst not in any thing injure the fame of my liberality. And that I may not appear more niggardly to thee than to others, remain with us as long as it pleaseth thee." The actor, seeing the charger full of mulberries, contrary to the season of the year, grew pale with wonder, and when he knew how it had happened, he cried out and said: "Truly there is none like thee among the kings of the earth munificent in thy liberality, and none like Kentigern, glorious in holiness, fearful in praises, doing wonders, who doeth such things in my sight beyond my expectation. Henceforth I will not leave thy house or thy service; but I will be unto thee a servant for ever as long as I live." The actor therefore remained at the King's court, and served him for many days as jester. Afterwards by the instigation of the fear of God, he set himself against his own face, gave up the profession of an actor, and, entering the ways of the better life, gave himself up to the divine service.

CHAPTER XXXVIII.

*Of the two vessels filled with milk which were sent by S. Kentigern to a
certain workman ; how the milk, when poured out into the river,
was formed into cheese.*

THERE was a certain man, skilled in the smith's craft, who
served by hammering and forging in the works of the man of
God, and in employments of the monastery, and received from
the Saint the necessary wages. Now, the Saint was wont to
use milk as food and drink, because, as we said above, he was
in the habit of abstaining from all liquor by which a man can
be intoxicated. He therefore ordered vessels full of new milk
to be carried to the smith, because he knew that workmen and
hired servants are gratified by partaking of the food prepared
for the lord and householder. But when the porter was crossing the river Clyde, the covers of the vessels accidentally
became open and all the milk was poured out into the water.
But strangely and wonderfully, the milk poured out did not
mix with the water, and was not changed either as to taste
or colour, but all at once became curdled and turned into
cheese. Not less properly was this cheese consolidated by the
beating of the waves than any other is wont to be by the
pressure of the hands. The porter snatched the little shape of
cheese from the water and went to the smith, to whom the
Saint had sent him, and related the whole matter to him.
Many saw this remarkable sign, and were amazed when they
saw how the fluid element was not turned into fluid or liquified.
But the smith and many others tasted of that cheese, and also
distributed little particles of the same, piece by piece, to
many to be kept as relics. Relics of this sort have been
received and preserved in many places and at many times,
and have declared the dear and famous merits of S. Kentigern, making them dearer and more famous still. But
although this sign bears much that is wonderful on the
face of it, yet to those who view it subtilly, and gather
spiritual things from corporeal, and invisible from visible, it
affords much instruction. In the milk, which fell into the water

but was not mixed with it or changed into water, or sunk in it,
it, we have an example of the preservation of innocence and
justice, which are relics to a peaceful man among those who
swell with pride, who sow to themselves many kinds of evil,
who seek to drown us with bad examples and persuasions,
who dissipate themselves in pleasure.   That the milk in the
stream was hardened into cheese gives us an example of
maintaining constancy under the pressure of tribulation and
difficulties.   For the just and the innocent hardens among the
waves as the milk did into cheese, when, in obedience to the
words proceeding out of the mouth of God, he perseveres in the
hard paths, and through many tribulations seeks to enter into
the kingdom of God.   And if he endures threats, insults,
losses, injuries from wicked and froward men, as if he did not
feel them, but in patience possesses his soul, and endeavours
to persevere in good, knowing of a surety that he who perseveres unto the end here, he shall be saved.

CHAPTER XXXIX.

*How S. Columba visited blessed Kentigern and saw a crown that came
down from heaven upon his head and a celestial light shining
around him.*

AT the time when Blessed Kentigern, placed in the Lord's
candlestick, like a lamp burning with heavenly desires, and
shining with life-giving words, in the examples of virtues and
with miracles of power, gave light to all who were in the
House of God, S. Columba, the Abbot, whom the Angles call
Columkillus, wonderful in doctrine and virtues, celebrated for
his presages of future events, yea rather, full of the spirit of
prophecy, and living in that glorious monastery which he had
built in the Island of Iona, desired earnestly not once but
continually to rejoice in the light of S. Kentigern.   For, hearing for a long time of the esteem in which he was held, he
desired to approach, visit, and behold him, and to come into

his closer intimacy, and to consult the sanctuary of his holy breast concerning the things which lay near to his own heart. And when the opportune moment came the holy Father Columba went forth, and a great crowd of disciples and others accompanied him, desiring to behold and look upon the face of so great a man. And when he approached the place which is called Mellindenor, where the Saint was then staying, he divided all his people into three bands, and sent a messenger before him to announce to the holy prelate his arrival and that of those who were with him.

The holy bishop rejoiced at the things which were told him concerning them, and calling to him his clergy and people, he, in like manner, divided them into three bands, and went forward with spiritual songs to meet them. In the forefront of the procession were placed the juniors in order of time, next the more advanced in years, then with himself there walked those who had grown old in good days, white and hoary, venerable in countenance, gesture, and bearing, yea, even in grey hairs. And all sang: "In the ways of the Lord, how great is the glory of the Lord." And again they answered : " The way of the just is made straight, and the path of the saints is prepared." On S. Columba's side they sang with tuneful voice: " The saints shall go from strength to strength : unto the God of gods every one of them shall appear in Sion," with Alleluia. Meanwhile some who had come with S. Columba asked him, saying, " Has S. Kentigern come in the first chorus of singers?" The Saint replied: "Not in the first, nor in the second, but in the third comes the genial bishop." And when they inquired how he knew this, he said : " I see a fiery pillar in fashion as of a crown of gold, set with sparkling gems, descending upon his head from heaven and a light of heavenly brightness encircling and shining around him as a veil, and covering him, and again returning to the skies. Wherefore it is given to me to know by this manifest sign that as Aaron he is the elect of God and sanctified ; who clothed with the light as with a garment and with a gold crown represented on his head appears to me with the sign of sanctity. When these two godlike men met, they embraced and kissed each other,

18

and having first satiated themselves with the spiritual banquet
of Divine words, they refreshed themselves with bodily food.
But how great was the sweetness of Divine contemplation
within their holy breasts is not for me to say, nor is it given to
me or to such as me to reveal the manna which is hidden and
which, methinks, is entirely unknown except to those who
taste it.

———

CHAPTER XL.

*Of the head of S. Kentigern's ram that was cut off and how it was
turned into stone.*

WHEN the two men we have just mentioned were mutually
joined together as two pillars in the court of the temple of the
Lord, firmly founded in faith and love and confirmed therein,
by the imitation and instructions of whom many peoples, tribes
and tongues have entered, and are still entering, into the
heavenly temple, which is the joy of the Lord, some sons of
the stranger who had come with S. Columba were hardened in
their evil habits and halted away from the paths of the man of
God.   For as the Ethiopian cannot change his skin, so he who
is accustomed to theft or rapine with difficulty changes his
malice.   There came, therefore, with Blessed Columba some
with no dovelike innocence, but merely by the advances of
their feet, with no affection of devotion and no progress in
morals.   While they journeyed they saw one of the flocks of
the holy bishop feeding in the distance, and leaving the path
and going by dark ways, as it is said in the Book of Proverbs
of such, they turned aside thither, and notwithstanding the
resistance and remonstrances of the shepherd, seized the
fattest wether.   But the shepherd in the name of the Holy
Trinity and by the authority of S. Kentigern forbade them to
commit such robbery, nay sacrilege, in the flock of the holy
prelate, admonishing them that if they would but ask a ram
from the Saint, they would without doubt receive one.   But one

of them drove away the shepherd, whom he insulted and even threatened with death, and took away a ram ; while the other taking out a knife cut off its head. They had debated how they should carry off the carcass with them, and, at a time and place suitable for their crime, skin and prepare it more carefully, as they well knew how, for their uses.

But a thing wonderful to relate, and yet more wonderful to behold, occurred. The ram with its head cut off ran back with marvellous speed to its own flock, and there fell down ; while its head, changed into stone, stuck firmly, as if fastened by some indissoluble glue, to the hands of him who held it and had struck it. Those who were able to pursue, catch, hold, and cut off the head of the ram when living and whole, now when it was beheaded were unable by following or pursuing to over- take it ; nor could they cast away the head, already become a stone, from their hands, though they tried with all their might. The men became rigid and their heart died within them and became as stone, as they were carrying a stone, and at length, taking wholesome counsel, they went to the Saints, and lying prostrate at the feet of S. Kentigern, penitent and suffused with tears, they besought him to forgive them. But the holy prelate, chiding them with gentle reproof, and warning them never again to presume to perpetrate fraud, theft, robbery, and, what is more detestable, sacrilege, unloosed them from the double bond, of sin and the hold of the stone. He ordered the carcase of the slain ram to be given to them and permitted them to depart. But the head which was turned into stone, remains there to this day as a witness to the miracle and, though mute, declares the merit of S. Kentigern.

Assuredly this miracle, as it seems to me, is, in the main, not inferior to that which the book of Genesis relates to have been wrought in the case of Lot's wife. After the avenger of the injury done to God, the fire from heaven was ordered to destroy the wicked subverters of the natural use of human generation and was already hanging over them, being instructed by an angelic oracle and assisted by its help, Lot escaped the fire of the overthrow and overwhelming of Sodom. But his wife, on looking back, contrary to the command given from heaven,

was changed into a rock, into an image of salt, to be a relish to
the food of brute animals. Here the head of a ram is trans-
muted into stone to condemn the hardness and cruelty of them
who carry off the property of others. In the figure of Lot's
wife, by the Lord's own teaching, every faithful man is taught
and warned not foolishly to draw back from any holy purpose
once taken in hand. In the head turned into stone every Christian is taught not to commit theft or fraud, or robbery or any
violence on the property of the Church or on the substance of
the servants of God. In the place where this miracle wrought
by S. Kentigern, in the sight of S. Columba and many others,
became known, they exchanged staves in pledge and testimony
of mutual love in Christ. The staff which S. Columba gave to
the holy bishop Kentigern was for a long time preserved in
the church of S. Wilfrid, bishop and confessor, at Ripon, and
on account of the sanctity of both the giver and receiver was
held in great reverence. Wherefore for some days these Saints
passed the time together conversing on the things which are of
God and on those which belong to the salvation of souls: after
bidding each other farewell in mutual love, they departed to
their own homes never to meet again.

CHAPTER XLI.

*How the man of God erected crosses in many places, by which even to
the present day miracles are wrought.*

THE venerable father and bishop Kentigern was in the habit
of erecting the triumphant standard of the Holy Cross in the
places where he had won the people to the dominion of Christ
by preaching and imbued them with the faith of the Cross
of Christ, or where he had dwelt for any length of time, that
all might learn that he was not in the least ashamed of the
Cross of our Lord Jesus Christ, which he carried on his forehead. But, as it seems to me, this very holy custom of the
holy man is in many ways supported by sound reason. Because the Saint was wont to erect this life-giving and holy and

terrible sign, in order that, as wax melts before the fire, so the enemies of the human race, the powers of the darkness of this world, melting away before this sign, might flow down, and terrified and routed, might flee afar off. It is fitting, moreover, that the soldiers of the Eternal King should recognise at a glance the invincible standard of their Commander, and flee to it, as to a tower of strength, from the face of the enemy and from the face of the wicked who afflict them, and that they may have that which they adore, and in which they boast before their eyes. And because, according to the Apostle, the wrestling against spiritual wickedness in high places and against the fiery darts of the evil one is continual, it is fit and healthful that they should fortify and protect themselves by signing themselves with this sign, and by imitating the passion of Christ, and with the Apostle bearing about in their bodies the prints of the wounds of Christ, crucify for the love of the Crucified One their own flesh with its vices and lusts and the world to them and themselves unto the world.

Among many crosses, therefore, which the man of God erected in divers places, there are two which to the present time work miracles. One in his own city of Glasgow he caused to be cut by quarriers from a block of stone of extraordinary size, which by the united exertions of many men and by the use of machines, he ordered to be set up in the cemetery of the Church of the Holy Trinity in which his episcopal chair is placed. But all their labour was spent in vain, every machine was powerless, human industry and strength were of no avail to erect it, though they toiled much and long. But when human ingenuity and help failed, the Saint had recourse to Divine aid. For on the following eve, which chanced to be Sunday, while the servant of Jesus Christ was pouring out prayers on behalf of this matter to the Lord, the Angel of the Lord descended from heaven and coming near, rolled back the stone cross and erected it in the place where it is to this day, and blessing it, signed it with the sign of the cross, hallowed it, and departed. The people, when they came to the church in the morning and discovered what had been done, were astonished and glorified God in his Saint. The cross was very large and from that time has never been wanting in great virtue. For many maniacs and those vexed with unclean spirits are wont to be tied to that cross on the night preceding the Lord's day and on the morrow they are found of a sound mind, delivered and cleansed, or sometimes dead or on the point of death.

Another cross, which it would be incredible to describe had it not been tested by sight and touch, he constructed merely of sea sand at Lothwerverd, while meditating justly and religiously on the Resurrection. In this place he remained for the space of eight years. Who ought to doubt that the Lord will not raise our mortal bodies, though they be resolved into dust, since He has so promised with His own blessed mouth, when in His name this Saint, of like passions with ourselves, raised up a cross from the sand of the sea while praying to the Lord? Truly, it ought to be believed by all that, at the Lord's will, the bones of the dead will be joined bone to his bone, according to the prophecy of Ezekiel, and that the Lord will give them sinews and make flesh to come upon them and skin to cover them and put breath into them and they shall live for ever, seeing that at the prayer of a man still mortal a mass of sand was condensed into a solid and perfect substance from the smallest particles, or as I may say atoms, and formed into a cross, which neither the burning sun by day nor the frost by night nor any inclemency of weather can dissolve. That cross therefore stands as a proof of our faith, showing that this corruptible must put on incorruption, and that the multitude of the children of Israel, though they be as the sand of the sea, a remnant shall be saved by the faith of the cross of Christ, and that the friends of God shall be multiplied beyond the number of the sand by Him who numbereth the stars of heaven, and the sand of the sea, and the drops of rain, and the days of the age. To this cross also many afflicted with divers diseases, and especially madmen and those vexed by the devil are bound in the evening and in the morning are often found safe and sound, and being set free return to their friends.

There are many other places in which he lived and especially during Lent, unknown to us, which the Saint sanctified by the presence of his holy indwelling Spirit. Yet many persons relate numerous instances regarding these which by some tokens diffuse his sanctity to this day, and by his merits afford to the infirm many blessings and have the efficacy of working miracles.

CHAPTER XLII.

How he tied up his chin with a certain bandage, and prepared for the departure of his soul.

BLESSED Kentigern, overcome by extreme old age, perceived from many rents in it that the ruin of his earthly house was at hand ; but the foundation of his faith, which was founded on a Rock, comforted his soul. For he trusted that when his earthly house of this tabernacle was dissolved, he had an house not made with hands prepared for him in heaven. And because both by reason of his extreme old age, and because he was touched with infirmity, the fastenings of his nerves throughout his whole body were almost entirely withered and loosened, he bound up his cheeks and chin with a certain linen bandage which went over the middle of his head and under his chin, neither too tight nor too loose. This the most refined man did, that by the falling of his chin nothing indecent might appear from the opening of his mouth, and that such a support might render him more ready in bringing forth what he could or would.

At length, this man, beloved by God and men, knowing that the hour approached when he should pass from this world to the Father of Lights, fortified himself with the sacred unction which is efficacious for the remission of sin and with the life-giving sacraments of the Lord's Body and Blood, in order that that ancient serpent seeking to bruise his heel should be unable to fix therein his poisonous tooth and inflict a deadly wound, but that with bruised head he might retreat in confusion. In

this way the Lord treading Satan under his feet, in order that
his holy soul might not be speedily confounded, when at his
going out from Egypt he spake with his enemies in the gate,
he waited patiently as hitherto, like an excellent under-pilot,
for the Lord who had saved him from the tempest of this age.
And now close to the shore, driven into the port of a certain
inward quiet by gentle navigation, after so many dangers of
the sea, he cast out the anchor of hope bound with the ropes of
his desires into the solid and sure ground, reaching of a truth even
within the veil, whither the Precursor, the Lord Jesus, entered
before him. Henceforth he awaited alone the departure from the
tents of Kedar and the entrance into the land of the living, so
that as a successful wrestler, he might in that City of The Virtues, that is, in the Heavenly Jerusalem, receive from the hand of
the Heavenly King the crown of glory and the diadem of the
Kingdom which fadeth not away. His own disciples gathered
around him he warned, as far as his strength permitted, concerning the observance of holy religion, the maintenance of
mutual charity and peace, the grace of hospitality, and of continuing instant in prayer and holy reading. But above all
things, he gave to them and left behind him short but peremp-
tory commands to avoid every evil appearance of simonia-
cal wickedness, to shun entirely the communion and society
of heretics and schismatics, and to observe strictly the decrees
of the holy Fathers, and especially the laws and customs of
Holy Church, the Mother of all. Then, as was meet, he gave
to each of them, as they humbly knelt before him, the kiss of
peace, and raising his hand, as best he could, he blessed them,
and bidding them a last farewell, he committed them all to the
care of the Holy Trinity and to the protection of the Holy
Mother of God, and gathered himself together, on that glorious
stony couch of his. Then one voice of mourners sounded everywhere; then fell as a horror of confusion deep sadness on the
face of all.

CHAPTER XLIII.

Of his disciples who sought a speedy journey to heaven, and of his warm bath.

BUT some of them, who loved the Saint of God more closely, prostrated themselves in tears before him and said : "We know, O Lord Bishop, that thou desirest to be dissolved and to be with Christ. For thine old age, venerable, very protracted and measured by the number of many years as well as thy spotless life demand it; but, we pray thee, have pity upon us whom thou hast begotten in Christ. For in whatsoever we have erred through human frailty we have always confessed it in thy presence, and have made amends, giving satisfaction to the judgment of thy discretion. Since then we have no power to retain thee any longer with us, seek from the Lord that it may be given to us to depart from this vale of tears to the joy of thy Lord with thee. For as to this we believe, even as we assert, that whatever thou askest the Divine Mercy will vouchsafe to thee, for the will of God has been to us directed in thy hand from thy youth. It seems to us improper that the bishop without his clergy, the pastor without any of his flock, the father without his sons, should enter into those festal and sublime places ; yea rather the more festal and sublime they are, the greater the company of his own that should attend him." And when they had urged many things in this way with tears, the man of God, overflowing with bowels of mercy, collecting his breath as well as he was able, said : "The will of God concerning us all be done ; let Him do with us as He knows best and as is well-pleasing to Him."

After these things the Saint was silent, and sighing in his soul for heaven awaited the passage of his spirit from the body ; and his disciples watching by him took care of him as of one nigh unto death. And behold, while the morning star, the herald of the dawn, the messenger of the light of day, tearing through the pall of the darkness of night, shone forth with flaming rays, the Angel of the Lord appeared in unspeakable splendour and the glory of God shone around him. For fear of him the guardians of the holy bishop were afraid and greatly amazed, and being but earthly vessels and unable to bear the weight of so great a glory they became as dead men. But the holy old man, comforted by the vision and the angelic visit, and forgetting as it were his age and infirmity and being made strong, experienced some foretastes of the blessedness now near at hand, and held close intercourse with the angel as with a most dear and familiar friend.

Now the heavenly messenger said to him these words : " O Kentigern, elect and beloved of God ! rejoice and be glad, and let thy soul magnify the Lord, since He has magnified His mercy toward thee. Thy prayer is heard, and the Divine ear has heard the preparation of thy heart. For it shall be to thee concerning the disciples who desire to accompany thee, as thou willest. Therefore be steadfast, and you shall see the help of the Lord toward you. On the morrow ye shall go forth from the body of this death to the unfailing life, and the Lord shall be with you and ye shall be with Him for ever. And because thy whole life in this world has been a perpetual martyrdom, it has pleased the Lord that thou shalt have an easier passage from life than other men. Cause to be prepared for thee therefore on the morrow a warm bath and going into it, thou shalt fall asleep in the Lord without pain, and therein rest in peace in Him. But after thou hast paid the debt of nature in it, immediately before the water cools, while it is yet warm about thee, let thy brethren enter after thee into this bath, and straightway loosed from the bonds of death they shall migrate with thee as the companions of thy journey, and being introduced into the splendours of the Saints, they shall enter with thee into the joy of thy Lord."

With these words the angelic vision and voice ceased, but a fragrance of marvellous and indescribable odour in some strange way spread through all the place and over all who were there. But the Saint calling his disciples to him, revealed to them in order the angelic mystery, and ordered his bath to be prepared as the Lord commanded by the angel. The brethren above mentioned gave unmeasured thanks to God Almighty and to their holy Father Kentigern, and assured of the oracle, in every

way they could, and fortified with the Divine Sacraments, they
prepared for what awaited them.

CHAPTER XLIV.

*How he passed out of this world and how he shone forth after his death
in many miracles.*

WHEN the octave of the Lord's Epiphany, on which the gentle
bishop himself had been wont every year to wash in sacred
baptism a multitude of people, was dawning—a day very acceptable to S. Kentigern and to the spirits of the sons of his
adoption, the Saint borne by their hands entered a vessel filled
with hot water which he had first hallowed with the sign of
salvation, and a circle of brethren standing round him waited
the issue of the event. And when the Saint had been some
little time in it, after raising his hands and eyes to heaven and
bowing his head, as if falling into a calm sleep, he yielded up
his spirit. For he seemed as free from the pain of death as he
stood forth spotless and pure from the corruptions of the flesh
and the snares of this world.

The disciples seeing what was taking place, lifted the holy
body out of the bath and eagerly strove with each other to
immerse themselves in it. And so, one by one before the
water cooled, they slept in great peace in the Lord, and having
tasted death with their father, the holy Bishop, they passed
with him to the heavenly mansions. And when the water had
become cold not only the fear of death but also every spark of
discomfort wholly disappeared.

This bath is in my opinion to be compared with the sheep-
pool in which, after the descent of the angel and the troubling
of the water, one sick man was healed of whatsoever infirmity
he had ; but he was still liable to death. But in this ablution
a very great company of Saints were cured of every sickness, to
live for ever with Christ. The water of that laver was distributed to divers persons in divers places ; and from its being

drunk or sprinkled health was conferred on many sick persons in many ways.

The brethren stripped the Saint of his ordinary clothes, which they partly preserved and partly distributed as precious relics, and clothed him in the sacred vestments which became so great a bishop. Then he was carried by the brethren into the choir with hymns and psalms, and the Life-giving Victim was offered to God for him by many. Diligently and most devoutly, as the custom of the Church at that time required, they celebrated his obsequies, and on the right side of the altar they laid beneath a stone with as much becoming reverence as they could, that home of virtues, that precious stone, by whose merit, as it was a time for collecting stones for the edifice of the heavenly temple, many elect and lively stones, along with that pearl, were taken up and laid in the treasuries of the Great King. The sacred remains of all the brethren were decently and separately consigned to the cemetery for sepulture in the order in which they followed the holy prelate from this world.

Blessed Kentigern therefore full of years, for he was a hundred and eighty-five years old, matured in merits, famous for signs, wonders and prophecies, on such wise passed from this world to the Father—from faith to sight, from labour to rest, from exile to the Fatherland, from the course to the crown of victory, from the present misery to the eternal glory. Blessed, I say, is the man to whom the heavens are open, who penetrated the sanctuary, who entered into the powers of the Lord, received by the angelic hosts, admitted into the ranks of the patriarchs and prophets, joined to the choirs of the Apostles, mingled in the ranks of the martyrs who are crowned with the purple of their rosy blood, associated with the sacred confessors of the Lord ; crowned with the snow-white choirs of virgins. And no wonder. For he was in office and merit an angel of the Lord who announced to those who were afar off and to them that were near peace and salvation in the blood of Jesus Christ ; his lips kept true wisdom, from his mouth many sought and found the law of God. He was also a prophet of the Highest, who knew many things which

were not, and foresaid and foretold many things to come.
Rightly moreover is he called and is the Apostle of the region
of Cambria, for its inhabitants and many other peoples are the
signs of his Apostleship. Deservedly also is he called a martyr
who in a constant and unceasing martyrdom mortifies himself
for Christ, and is proved to have had his heart prepared for
every kind of death if the occasion had offered. For, for the
name of Christ and for the defence of truth and righteousness
he frequently offered himself to persecution, proscription, the
snares and swords of the enemies of the cross of Christ, and
bravely, and happily triumphed over the world, the flesh, and
the devil and his satellites. He by change of name is called
the Confessor of Christ, who confessing the name of Christ
before peoples and Kings, confidently preached, and invited all
men to the profession of the name of Christ, and to the confession of the Christian Faith, of the praise of God and of
their own sin.

Moreover by a certain special prerogative he obtained a
virginal honour and glory, who from the tamarisk extracted
balsam, from the nettle the lily, and while in the vessel of this
fragil and frail body never disturbed, as they say, even by a
look his angelic celibacy, and preserved in a vessel of clay the
heavenly treasure of chastity. Wherefore from a virgin body
he soared in white to the white-robed company, that without
spot he might stand before the throne of God and the Lamb,
and following Him whithersoever He goeth, sing the new
song, unknown to all save to those who have not defiled their
garments. Justly, therefore, that holy man lives as a companion, fellow-citizen and partaker with all the Saints, who in
this life had communion with all Saints, and always sought to
please, obey and follow and to be united in spirit with the
Saint of all Saints, the Sanctifier of all, and being united to
them, lives and rejoices with Him now and for ever.

The spirit of S. Kentigern being translated to the starry
realms, that which the earth, the mother of all, had bestowed,
she gathered into her womb. Nevertheless the power of
miracles, which grew in him when living, could not be buried
beneath the turf or hid by the stony mound, but burst forth.

For from the day of his burial down to the present, his sacred bones are known to have there germinated into very many miracles, and they do not cease to announce, by benefits bestowed in respect to many kinds of infirmities, that both in heaven and on earth the just is had in everlasting remembrance. At his tomb sight is restored to the blind, hearing to the deaf, the power of walking to the lame, speech to the dumb, cleanness of skin to the leprous, strength of limb to the paralytic, sense to the insane. The impious, the sacrilegious, the perjured, violators of the peace of his Church and profaners of the holy place are justly punished.

Moreover on one occasion a certain man by night stole away from Glasgow a cow which in the morning was found living and bound to the foot of the thief who was dead, which struck him who sought it with both astonishment and joy. Likewise many, who, though guilty of sins of the flesh, did not hesitate to pollute the holy place with their impure steps, were sometimes punished with sudden death, often mutilated, and at times visited with some incurable and protracted disease in their limbs. Thus also the breakers of his peace often suffered. Many, likewise, have often experienced in themselves the punishment of their sin, who have presumed by any servile work to dishonour the festival of the Saint, during which at the Church in Glasgow, where his most sacred body rests, a great multitude is wont to assemble from divers parts, to seek his intercession and to behold the miracles which are here wont to be wrought.

CHAPTER XLV.

Of the prophecy of a certain man, and of the burial of the Saints in Glasgow.

IN the same year that S. Kentigern was freed from earthly things and migrated to the heavens, King Rederech, who has been so often named, remained much longer than usual in the royal town which is called Pertnech (Partick). In his court there lived a certain fool called Laloecen, who received the necessaries of food and clothing from the munificence of the King. For the chiefs of the earth, the sons of the kingdom, are given to vanity and are wont to retain men of this kind about them, who by their foolish words and gestures may excite to jokes and laughter the lords themselves and their household. This man after the death of S. Kentigern gave himself up to the heaviest grief and would not receive consolation from any one.

When they asked him why he mourned so inconsolably, he answered that his lord King Rederech and another of the chiefs of the land, Morthec by name, would not continue long in this life after the death of the holy Bishop, but would die during the present year. That the saying of the fool was uttered not foolishly but rather prophetically, the death of those whom he mentioned within the same year clearly proved. Nor is it much to be marvelled at, that the Creator of all things allowed to be announced by the mouth of a fool what had been determined of the Lord, since even Balaam, the soothsayer, by His inspiration foresaw many and great things in his seer's mind and foretold them, and Caiaphas prophesied that the redemption of the people would come from the death of Christ, and by the mouth of a she-ass the madness of a prophet was rebuked, and the destruction of Jerusalem was foretold by the mouth of a madman, as Josephus writes. So in the same year that the holy Bishop Kentigern passed away, the King and Prince aforesaid died, and were buried in Glasgow.

In the cemetery of the Church of this city as the inhabitants and countrymen assert, 665 saints rest, and all the great men of that region have long been wont to be buried there. O how much is that place to be feared and to be had in reverence, which so many pledges of the Saints adorn as their resting-place! which so precious a Confessor decorates with his sacred spoils, and illustrates with so many miracles that if all were committed to writing they would be seen to fill great volumes. Not only in the place where he rests in the body, though there more frequently, and especially on his anniversary, is he used to shine forth in signs, but in almost all places in which he is had in remembrance, in churches and chapels, and at altars, he is present as a most powerful helper in necessities to those placed in tribulations, to those who love him, trust in him, cry to him.   And where faith or some reason demands it, he does not cease to shine in miracles to the praise and glory of our Lord Jesus Christ; whose is the glory, praise, honour and power, for ever and ever.   Amen.

Thus endeth the Life of the Most Holy Kentigern, Bishop and Confessor, who is also called Mungu.

THE LIFE OF S. SERVANUS.

THE LIFE OF SERVANUS.

CHAPTER I.

THERE was a certain noble king in the land of Canaan by by name Obeth, the son of Eliud ; and the name of his wife was Alfia, the daughter of the King of Arabia. They lived together twenty years but had no offspring. Therefore they very frequently besought God and offered unto Him oblations and sacrifices that He would grant unto them a worthy child, in order that their reproach might be taken away. For this cause the King ordained through all His kingdom that all men from the least unto the greatest should fast three days and three nights and earnestly entreat the pity of God for the King and Queen, that the shame of sterility might be turned away from them. On the third night, at the last crowing of the cock, the angel of the Lord suddenly appeared to the King in a dream as he slept, saying: "Go to the city which is called Heliopolis and in it thou shalt find a very beautiful fountain and in it bathe three times. Afterwards you shall have what you desire." And departing, they came to the aforesaid fountain and did according to the saying of the angel. And the Queen desiring an herb growing by the fountain, which is called mandragon, she ate of it. After she had eaten thereof her husband went in unto her and she conceived. On the following night the angel appeared unto the Queen comforting her, and saying : " Be not sad nor sorrowful, O Queen ! for lo, thou bearest in thy womb two sons who shall excel in faith and works. The name of the one shall be Generatius ; that is, Shining Gem, and he shall be a great king over all the land of the Canaanites. The name of the other shall be Malachias or Servanus. And after

he has finished the course of this secular life, these names will
prove to have suited him well. For Malachias being interpreted is Angel of the Lord. This is a fit name for him, in
that he lived as the ambassador of the Apostolic see, pro-
claiming the Word of God to the four quarters of the world.
But he is called Servanus from serving God, in that he served
our Lord Jesus Christ, labouring in every good work night and
day." After saying these words the angel departed, and the
Queen awoke and told her husband the words of the angel.
Both therefore rejoiced and gave great thanks to God.

CHAPTER II.

AFTER the boy was born he was taken to the Bishop of the
city of Alexandria, Mayonius by name, to be baptized by him.
The Bishop baptized him and gave him the name Servanus.
Blessed Servanus was accordingly nurtured seven years ; and
his father died. Now when his father was dead, they conferred
upon him the government of the whole of their kingdom. But
he, cleaving to God from his youth, opposed all their wishes ;
and his brother Generatius reigned in his stead.   Now S.
Servanus went to the city of Alexandria to devote himself
there to divine study and to learn the arts.   And there he remained thirteen years and received the habit of a monk from
the bishop of that city.   After thirty years, he was earnestly
advised by the aforenamed Bishop that he ought to be promoted to sacred orders, inasmuch as he was deserving. Accordingly he was advanced to the order of the priesthood, though
unwilling and gainsaying. Now after he was ordained he came
into his own land, and all the Canaanites elected him with
great joy to the bishopric.   That bishopric he ruled in peace
for twenty years, building monasteries and churches in it,
and serving God day and night.   Then the angel of the Lord
came to him, saying : " Thou art commanded by the Lord
God to go out and depart from thy country and from thy
kindred." Blessed Servanus answered : " Freely will I go,

but I know not whither my Lord desires me to go." The
angel on this said to blessed Servanus : " I will be with thee
whithersoever thou goest, delivering thee from every temptation of the devil ; and I will be thy companion, prospering
the way of thy journey on sea and on land, from this day until
the day of the dissolution of thy body." Then S. Servanus
took leave of all the clerics and laity of his see and of his
kindred and his friends, and blessed them. But they, lamenting his departure, earnestly besought him that he would not
send them away desolate. But he, heeding not their tears
and prayers, took his journey with a great multitude of companions, the angel guiding him.

CHAPTER III.

S. SERVANUS, afterwards, with fifty and ten thousand, came to
the bank of the river Nile, and with all his company he safely
crossed the river. Next, he arrived with them at the shore of
the Red Sea, and they all crossed that sea with dry feet. Then
after two months he came to the city of Jerusalem, and was
there the honourable patriarch for seven years, in the place of
James the Bishop, patriarch of the people of Jerusalem. Now,
on a certain day the Angel said to S. Servanus ; " Ascend
Mount Sion, and go round about it." S. Servanus ascended
Mount Sion and went round about it. There was shown to
him the tree from which the health-bringing Cross of Christ
was hewn. Then the Angel said unto him :—" Cut from this
tree four staves and carry them away with thee, and they shall
be held in great virtue and reverence after you." At the voice
of the Angel S. Servanus cut three staves. But the wood for
a larger staff the Angel himself cut off and handed it to S.
Servanus, and entrusted it to him. Thereafter the Saint held
and preserved this staff in the greater honour and reverence.
After these things he returned to Jerusalem with joy. And
there the Angel said to him :—" It is time to leave this city

and to go to the city of Constantinople, for this place is near
to thy country and kindred." Blessed Servanus therefore arose
and blessed all the inhabitants of Jerusalem, taking leave of
them.   After this he came to Constantinople with all the
multitude of his companions, and was there honourably entertained for three years.   Then being warned by the same
Angel, he came to the land and to the island of Salvatoris.
Now the island is called Salvatoris because in it our Saviour
graciously came to us.   Afterwards he came to Rome with a
very great company.   And the Romans learning his fame,
which was noised abroad through all the countries and regions
round about, received him with great honour.   Now in these
days the Romans were without a Pope and without a teacher.
But the assembly of the clergy and people of Rome chose him
to the Apostolate.   And he was thus in the chair of Peter,
ruling and teaching the Roman people, and doing signs and
wonders seven years.

CHAPTER IV.

THE Angel of the Lord speaks with S. Servanus, saying, "Thy
God commandeth thee to go out from this place, for it is too
pleasant for thee to be here." Then Blessed Servanus addressed
the Roman clergy and people, saying ;—" Men, brethren, I
take leave of you all and leave you all my benediction.   For
it behoves me, being warned of the Lord, to go into distant
parts and to obey the Lord Jesus Christ in all things." On
hearing this all the Romans were greatly displeased, for all
the Roman people were of one mind to go with him, because
they greatly loved a man so glorious in doctrine, manner and
nobility.   For they would rather endure hardness and privation
in wandering through the world with him than be deprived of
his presence and mellifluous doctrine.   Nevertheless, he departed from the city of Rome with a great multitude of clergy
and of the people, both men and women, sorrowing greatly

over his departure, and came to the Hill of Tears. Blessed
Servanus stood in this place, and turning to the people, said :
" Men, brethren, and people beloved of God, grieve not over
my departure nor be sorrowful, but divide yourselves into two
companies ; let one remain here at Rome ; let the other lay
aside all worldly care and follow me in this pilgrimage ; for
those who remain and for those who come with us I will pray
God that He Himself may be with you, pardoning all your
sins, and that He may have mercy upon us." All responded,
" Amen." And the companies were separated and he blessed
them with tears, and kissing them, said,—" Farewell, and abide
in Christ."

CHAPTER V.

NOW after Blessed Servanus with all his company ascends the
Alps, he comes to the valley which is called Nigra, or the
Valley of Beasts. And because Servanus knew that during
that night he would be tempted of the devil, he passed the
night in that valley. Then the angel said to the blessed man :
" I make known to thee the pains which thou and all thine are
about to suffer this night." And he said to him : " Comfort
the crowds, and say to them that when the pains and torments
of this night are passed, they will no more suffer the pains of
hell." After this the angel departed, and S. Servanus came to
the crowd, and comforting them, said : " Strengthen yourselves,
and be ready to endure the pains which will this night come
upon you." He set a verse before them as an example of
prophecy, viz. : " Thou shalt tread on the asp, and the basilisk
and the lion and the dragon shalt thou trample under foot."
That is, You shall all, if you persevere in the faith of the
Holy Trinity, tread on the asp and the basilisk, that is,
on the devil and his pomps, and nothing shall harm you.
Then the Saint said : " Eat and prepare yourselves for
the coming wars." Now when they had finished eating

and had repeated the verse, immediately there came a most black thick darkness over the valley in which they were. Then there came great earthquakes, thunders and lightnings, hail and sulphurous fires ; and divers kinds of beasts, two-footed and four-footed, filled the valley round about them. Then came gnats having horny beaks, dragons, winged serpents, and every torment which the Prince of Darkness can show to man. When they saw all these things, great part of the crowd died. But S. Servanus, seeing that his companions were un-able to endure these things, arose and blessed the valley, when all vanished and returned to nothing, and did no more hurt to any one. Then S. Servanus came with seven thousand thous-ands to the Ictean Sea which separates England from France, and they crossed it dry-shod. Thus God granted them a way and support on the sea. And afterwards he went from place to place until he came to the stream which is called the Forth. Now S. Edhennanus (Adamnan) was abbot in Scotland at that time, and he went to meet Servanus as far as the island of Keth (Inchkeith), and received him with great veneration be-cause he had heard much good concerning him. When the space of one night was passed there, and after a time which it pleased them to enjoy in sweet conversation, S. Servanus said : " How shall I dispose of my household and companions ? " S. Adamnan replied : " Let them dwell in the land of Fife and from the sea of the Britains as far as the mountain which is called Okhel." And so it was done.

CHAPTER VI.

AFTERWARDS S. Servanus, with only a hundred companions in his train, came to Kinel, and threw the branch which he held across the sea, and from it there grew an apple tree, which among the moderns is called Monglas. Then the Angel said to the blessed man : " There where that very beautiful tree has grown shall be the resting place of thy

body." S. Servanus then came to the place which is called
Culenros (Culross), desiring to dwell there, and cleared away all
the thorns and thickets which abounded in the place. But the
King of Scotia, namely, Brude, son of Dagart, who then held
the kingdom of the Picts, was greatly enraged because without
his permission he was dwelling there. Now the King sent his
spearmen to slay S. Servanus with his whole household. Meanwhile a violent disease had attacked the King so that he had
well nigh given up the ghost. He therefore hastily sent to the
Saint of the Lord. The sick King spoke to the Saint as he
came, saying : " O Saint of God, for the sake of Christ in
whom thou believest, restore me to health and thou shalt have
the place in which you dwell as a perpetual gift." The Saint,
moved with the prayers and piety of the King, restored him to
health. S. Servanus after this founded and dedicated a cemetery and his own Church in Culenros. The time there being
fulfilled, he went to the island of Leven that he might speak
with S. Adamnan in person. Now S. Adamnan joyfully received the blessed man with honour, and thinking that he was
seeking a place suitable for his religion, yielded that island to
him as a gift with good will. Servanus therefore abode in it
seven years, founded a monastery, and won many souls.
Thence departing, he traversed and went round all the region
of Fife, raising divers divine edifices to the Most High Creator.

CHAPTER VII.

ON a certain occasion S. Servanus was in the cave at Dysart,
and a certain brother, a monk, who was with him and was sick,
desired a drink of wine and could not get one. Then Blessed
Servanus took water from the fountain which is there and
blessed it and changed the water into wine, and the sick man
was healed. Moreover in that cave when S. Servanus was
lying upon his couch after matins, the devil came to him,
tempting him and disputing with him. And he said to him,

"Art thou a wise cleric, Servanus?" "What wishest thou O most miserable of all creatures?" The devil said: "I wish to dispute with thee and to question thee a little?" S. Servanus said: "Begin thou miserable wretch, begin." Satan asked him: "Where was God before He created the heavens and the earth, and before all the creatures were made?" Blessed Servanus said to him: "In Himself: for He is not local, and is held by no place, neither is He divided, nor subject to the motions of time, but is whole everywhere." And the devil said: "Why did God create creatures?" The Saint said: "Because there cannot be a Creator without creatures." "Wherefore did He make them very good?" To this the Saint replied: "Because God did not wish to do evil, or lest He should seem envious by being unwilling that aught should be good except Himself." The devil said: "Where did God form Adam?" The Saint said: "In Hebron." Satan said: "Where was he afterwards cast out from Paradise?" The Saint said: "Where he was formed." Satan said: "How long was he in Paradise after he had sinned?" The Saint replied: "Only seven hours." Satan said: "Why did God permit Adam and Eve to sin in Paradise?" To this the Saint replied: "Because God foresaw what great thing would come thereof. For Christ had not been born according to the flesh, had not Adam and Eve sinned." Satan said: "Why could not Adam and Eve be set free of themselves?" Servanus to this replied: "Because they did not fall of themselves, but through another, that is through the Devil persuading them. Therefore by another, that is Christ, born of their own stock they were set free." "Why did not God make a new man and send him to deliver the human race?" The Saint said: "Because he would not have pertained to us unless he had been of the race of Adam." "Why are you men delivered by the Passion of Christ, and not we demons?" "Because we have not the origin of our fall in ourselves, but from you demons? But as for you demons, because you are not of a fragile nature nor desire to repent and have contracted the origin of sin in yourselves, the Passion of Christ does not avail for you." The Devil therefore seeing

that he could do nothing against the true Saint, and being
vanquished in the interrogation, said : " Thou art wise Servanus, and I can dispute no more with thee." Servanus responded : " Go thou wretched creature, go and quickly depart
hence, and never more venture to appear in this place to any
man." And that place in honour of the holy, holy, holy
Servanus, has been sacred up to this present day.

CHAPTER VIII.

MOREOVER, on a certain occasion blessed Servanus was at
Tuligbotuan (Tillicoultry), and an evil spirit entered into a
certain miserable man so that he had such a desire to eat, that
he could in no wise be satisfied.   S. Servanus placed his
thumb in his mouth, and the devil crying out terribly came out
of him and left him. On another occasion Blessed Servanus
was in the same place, and a certain poor little woman brought
forth two dead sons there, and bore them to blessed Servanus,
and with tears besought him to restore them to life for her.
But the Saint prostrated himself on the ground, and entreated
our Lord God to look upon this woman, and in love to restore
to her her offspring alive. Accordingly, God hearkened unto
the prayer of the holy man, and restored to the mother both
her children alive. On another night the same Saint was at
Alva, being entertained by a certain poor peasant who had no
substance, except one pig, which he killed that night for the
holy man, and when he rose on the morrow, he found it alive
in his yard. At another time there was a man in Aitheren
who had a sheep which he loved and nourished in his house.
But a thief coming stealthily stole it away from him. Now
the ram was sought through the whole parish, and was not
found, and lo! when the thief was brought into the presence
of the blessed man and interrogated by the Saint whether he
was guilty of the crime laid to his charge, he affirmed on oath
that he was not. And beginning again to swear by the staff

of the holy man, the wether bleated in his bowels. And the wretch confessed his sin, and asked and received pardon from S. Servanus.

At the time when the Saint was in the cell at Dunning, it was told him that a dragon great and terrible and very loathesome, whose look no mortal could endure, had come into his city. The Saint went out to meet it, and taking his staff in his right hand, fought with the dragon in a certain valley and slew it. From that day that valley is called the Dragon's Den. After these things there came to Blessed Servanus from the Alps three blind men and three lame men and three deaf men, who had been told that if they came to Blessed Servanus in Scotland, they would be healed. Therefore when they came they addressed the holy man, saluting him, and revealed to him the reason of their great labour and journey, and earnestly besought him to cure them of their infirmities. But the holy man, fearing that they said these things for the purpose of tempting him, spoke to them saying: " Men, brethren, think you I am God, or do you tempt me beyond what you see in me when you ask this great thing from me that I should heal you?" But they, prostrating themselves at his feet and bursting into tears, said with an oath: " No, lord father, no ; but we believe that thy prayers and petitions avail much with God, and that we can obtain health through thee from the great Creator." Blessed Servanus, therefore, hearing their faith, blessed a certain fountain, and made them wash in it three times. And they, coming out thence, were made sound through the merit of the holy man. And thus the most holy Servanus gave sight to the blind, the power of walking to the lame, and hearing to the deaf. To these and to many others suffering divers kinds of diseases, he, through the power of God, gave and furnished health. Afterwards this Saint, beloved brethren, was assailed by a grievous infirmity, and was held down by the virulence of fever, and called all his brethren and announced to them that the day of his dissolution was near. Then the brethren wept much, and continuing instant in prayer to God for him, responded : " Why dost thou desert us, O Father? or to whom wilt thou leave us desolate ones? For we would rather die with thee than live in the world without thee." But the holy man, after many miracles, after divers works, after founding many churches in Christ, when he had bestowed peace on the brethren, in the cell at Dunning, on the first day of the Kalends of July, gradually yielded up his spirit and commended it to the Great Creator. After his death his disciples and well nigh all the people of the whole province conveyed his corpse to Culross. And there, with psalms and hymns and chantings, they interred him honourably, where his merits and the virtues of his merits flourish unto this day, to the praise and honour of Almighty God, who in the perfect Trinity liveth and reigneth for ever and ever. Amen.

THE LIFE OF S. MARGARET,
QUEEN OF SCOTLAND.

THE LIFE OF S. MARGARET.

PROLOGUE.

To the honourable and excellent Matilda, Queen of the English, T[urgot], a servant of the servants of S. Cuthbert, sends the blessing of peace and health in this present life, and in the life which is to come the blessing of all good things.

FORASMUCH as you have requested, you have also commanded me, to present to you in writing the story of the life of your mother, whose memory is held in reverence, and of whose life, which was well pleasing to God, you have often heard by the concordant praise of many. You are wont to say that in this matter my testimony is especially trustworthy, since you have understood that by reason of her frequent and familiar intercourse with me I am acquainted with the most part of her secrets. These your commands and desires I willingly obey; obeying them I greatly venerate them, and venerating them I congratulate you, that, having been appointed by the King of the Angels, Queen of the English, you desire not only to hear about the life of the Queen, your mother, who ever longed for the Kingdom of the Angels, but also to look upon it in writing continually, so that, although you were but slightly acquainted with her face, you may at least obtain a more perfect knowledge of her virtues. My own wish, indeed, is to fulfil your commands, but I am wanting, I must own, in the ability; the materials for this undertaking being, in sooth, much greater than I am able either by speech or writing to set forth.

2. Thus I am in a strait between two, and am drawn hither and thither. On account of the greatness of the undertaking I fear to obey; and on account of the authority of you who

command, and the memory of her of whom I am to speak, I dare not refuse. But, though I am unable to treat so great a subject in the manner it deserves to be treated, I am nevertheless bound, as far as in me lies, to make it known. I owe this to the love I have for her and to the obedience which is due to your command. The grace of the Holy Spirit, which gave such efficacy to her virtues, will vouchsafe help to me, I trust, to narrate them. "The Lord shall give the word to them that preach good tidings with great power," and again, "Open thy mouth wide and I will fill it." For no man can fail in the Word who believes in the Word. "In the beginning was the Word, and the Word was God." In the first place, therefore, I desire that you, and that through you others, should know that if I were to attempt to relate all that could be told respecting her, I should be thought to be flattering you under cover of your mother's praises on account of the greatness of your queenly dignity. But far be it from my grey hairs to mingle the crime of falsehood with the virtues of such a woman, in setting forth which, I profess, God is my Witness and Judge, that I add nothing to the truth; but suppress many things lest they should seem incredible, and that I may not be said, as the orator has it, to be decking out a crow with the colours of a swan.

CHAPTER I.

Her noble descent and virtues as a Queen and as a Mother.

MANY, as we read, have derived the origin of their name from a quality of the mind, so that there is shewn in respect to them a correspondence between the word of their name and the grace they have received. Thus Peter was so named from "the Rock," that is Christ, on account of the firmness of his faith; so John, that is "the grace of God," because of his contemplation of the Divinity and his prerogative of the Divine love; and the sons of Zebedee were called Boanerges, that is, the Sons of Thunder, because they thundered forth the preaching of the Gospel. The same was true of this virtuous woman, in whom the fairness indicated by her name was surpassed by the exceeding beauty of her soul. She was called Margaret, *i.e.* a Pearl, and in the sight of God she was esteemed a goodly pearl by reason of her faith and good works. She was a pearl indeed to you, to me, to us all, yea even to Christ ; and because she was Christ's, she is all the more ours, now that she has left us and is taken to the Lord. This pearl I say was taken from the dunghill of this world and now shines in her place among the jewels of the Eternal King. This I think no one will doubt, when he has read the following account of her life and death. When I recall the conversations I had with her, seasoned as they were with the salt of wisdom, when I think of the tears wrung from her by the compunction of her heart, when I consider the sobriety and staidness of her manners and remember her affability and prudence, I rejoice while I lament, and while lamenting I rejoice. I rejoice, because she has passed away to God after whom she longed ; I lament, because I am not rejoicing with her in the heavenly places. I rejoice for her, I say, because she now sees in the land of the living the goodness of the Lord in which she believed ; but for myself I mourn, because as long as I suffer the miseries of this mortal life in the land of the dead, I am daily compelled to cry, " O wretched man that I am, who shall deliver me from the body of this death ? "

4. Since, then, I am to speak of that nobility of mind which she had in Christ, it is fitting that something should be first said of that nobility by which she was also distinguished according to this world. Her grandfather was King Edmund, who, because he was strong in battle and invincible by his enemies, derived his distinctive name from the excellence of his valour, for he was called in English Ironsides. His brother on his father's side, but not on his mother's, was the most religious and meek Edward, who proved himself the Father of his Country ; and as another Solomon, that is, a lover of peace, protected his kingdom by peace rather than by arms. He had a mind that subdued anger, despised avarice, and was entirely

free from pride. And no wonder; for as he derived the glory
of his kingly rank from his ancestors, so also he derived from
them, as by hereditary right, the nobility of his life; being
descended from Edgar, King of the English, and from Richard,
Count of the Normans, his grandfathers on either side, men
who were not only most illustrious, but also most religious.
Of Edgar, in order to describe how great he was in this world
and what he was in Christ, it may be briefly said that he was
marked out beforehand both as a King and as a lover of justice and peace. For at his birth S. Dunstan heard the holy
angels rejoicing in heaven and singing with great joy: "Let
there be peace, let there be joy in the Church of the English,
as long as this new-born boy shall hold the kingdom and
Dunstan runs the course of this mortal life."

5. Richard, also, the father of Emma, the mother of this
Edward, was an illustrious ancestor worthy of so noble a
grandchild. He was a man of the greatest energy, and
deserving of every praise. None of his forefathers ruled the
earldom of Normandy with greater prosperity and honour, or
were more fervent in their love of religion. Endowed with
great riches, like a second David, he was poor in spirit;
exalted to be lord over his people, he was a lowly servant of
the servants of Christ. Among other things which he did as
memorials of his love of religion, this devout worshipper of
Christ built that noble monastery of Fecamp, in which he was
often wont to reside with the monks, and where, in the habit
of a secular but in heart a monk, he used to place the food of
the brethren on the table when they were eating their silent
meal, and serve them with drink; so that, according to the
Scripture, "The greater he was the more he humbled himself
in all things." If any one wishes to know more fully his
works of magnificence and virtue, let him read the *Acts of the
Normans*, which contains his history. From ancestors so
renowned and illustrious, Edward, their grandchild, did in no
wise degenerate. On the father's side only, as was before said,
he was the brother of King Edmund, from whose son came
Margaret, who by the splendour of her merits completes the
glory of this illustrious family.

6. While therefore Margaret was still in the flower of her youth, she began to lead a life of great strictness, to love God above all things, to occupy herself with the study of the Holy Scriptures, and to exercise her mind therein with joy. Keen penetration of intellect was hers to understand any matter whatever it might be, tenacity of memory to retain many things, and a graceful facility of language to give expression to her thoughts. While therefore she meditated in the law of the Lord day and night, and, like another Mary, sitting at His feet, she delighted to hear His word, by the desire of her friends rather than by her own, yea, rather by the appointment of God, she was married to Malcolm, son of Duncan, the most powerful King of the Scots. But though compelled to do the things which are of the world, she deemed it beneath her to set her affections upon them ; for she delighted more in good works than in abundance of riches. With things temporal she procured for herself everlasting rewards ; for in heaven where her treasure was, there she had placed her heart. And because before all things she sought the kingdom of God and His righteousness, the abundant grace of the Almighty freely added to her honours and riches. All things which became the rule of a prudent Queen were done by her ; by her advice the laws of the kingdom were administered ; by her zeal the true religion was spread and the people rejoiced in the prosperity of their affairs. Nothing was more firm than her faith, more constant than her favour, more enduring than her patience, weightier than her counsel, more just than her decisions, or more pleasant than her conversation.

7. After she had attained this high dignity, she at once, in the place where her nuptials were celebrated, built an eternal monument of her name and devotion. For she erected the noble church there in honour of the Holy Trinity with a threefold purpose ; for the redemption of the King's soul, for the good of her own, and to obtain prosperity in this life and in the life that is to come for her children. This church she adorned with divers kinds of precious gifts, among which, as is well known, were vessels not a few of solid and pure gold for
- the holy service of the altar, of which I can speak with the

greater certainty, since by the Queen's commands, I myself
for a long time had them all under my charge there. A cross,
also, of incomparable value, having upon it an image of the
Saviour which she had caused to be covered with a vestment
of purest gold and silver studded with gems, she placed there,
which proves to those who behold it even now the earnestness
of her faith. To this the Church of St. Andrews bears witness,
where is preserved, as is seen to this day, a most beautiful
crucifix which she erected there. Without these things, those,
I mean, which belong to the celebration of the divine service,
her chamber was never found ; it seemed, so to say, to be the
workshop of a heavenly artificer. There were always to be
seen in it copes for the cantors, chasubles, stoles, altar-cloths,
also other priestly vestments and church ornaments. Some
were in course of preparation, others, already finished, were of
admirable beauty.

8. With these works women of noble birth and approved
gravity of conduct who were deemed worthy to be engaged in
the Queen's service, were entrusted. No men were admitted
among them, save such as she allowed to accompany her when
she sometimes paid them a visit. There was no unseemly
familiarity among them with the men, nor any pert frivolity.
For the Queen united such strictness to her sweetness and
such sweetness to her strictness that all who were in her service, men as well as women, while fearing loved her and while
loving feared her. Wherefore in her presence no one ventured
to do anything wrong, or even to utter an unseemly word.
For repressing all evil in herself, there was great gravity in her
joy and something noble in her anger. Her mirth was never
expressed in immoderate laughter ; when angry she never
gave way to fury. Always angry with her own faults, she
sometimes reproved those of others with that commendable
anger tempered with justice which the Psalmist enjoined, when
he says : " Be angry and sin not." Her whole life, regulated
with the utmost skill of discretion, was, as it were, a pattern of
the virtues. Her conversation was seasoned with the salt of
wisdom : her silence was filled with good thoughts. Her
bearing so corresponded with the gravity of her character that

she might be believed to have been born simply to show what comeliness of life is. But to speak briefly, in whatever she was wont to say or do, she showed that her mind was dwelling on things divine.

9. Nor did she spend less pains upon her children than upon herself, that they might be brought up with the utmost care, and especially that they might be trained in virtue. Hence because she knew the Scripture : He that spareth the rod hateth his child, she instructed the governor of the nursery as often as the children fell into such faults as are common to their age, to curb them with threats and the rod. By reason of their mother's religious care they excelled many who were of greater age in their good behaviour. Among themselves they were always kindly and peaceable, and the younger everywhere paid respect to the elder. Hence, also, during the celebration of the Mass, when they went up after their parents to make their offerings, the younger never in any way presumed to precede the older, but the older were wont to go before the younger according to their age. She would often call them to her, and, as far as their age would allow, instruct them concerning Christ and the faith of Christ, and carefully endeavour to admonish them to always fear Him. "O my children," she would say, "fear the Lord ; for they that fear Him shall not want anything that is good ; and if you love Him, He will give you, my darlings, prosperity in this life and eternal felicity with all the saints." This was the mother's desire, her admonition, the prayer which she uttered day and night with tears for her little ones, that they might acknowledge their Maker in the faith that worketh by love, and acknowledging worship Him, and worshipping Him, love Him in all things and above all things, and loving Him attain to the glory of the heavenly kingdom.

CHAPTER II.

Her care for the honour of the Kingdom and discipline of the Church.
Abuses corrected.

NOR need we wonder that the Queen ruled herself and her household wisely, since she was always guided by the most wise counsel of the Holy Scriptures. For what I used frequently to admire in her was that amid the distraction of lawsuits, and the countless affairs of the Kingdom, she gave herself with wonderful diligence to the reading of the Word of God, concerning which she used to ask profound questions of the learned men who were sitting near her. But as among them no one had a profounder intellect, so no one had the power of clearer expression. Thus it often happened that these teachers left her much more learned than when they came. She had a religious and earnest desire for the sacred volumes, and very often her affectionate familiarity with me urged me to exert myself to obtain them for her. Nor in these things was she anxious for her own salvation alone ; she sought also that of others. And first of all, with the help of God, she made the King himself most attentive to works of justice, mercy, almsgiving, and other virtues. From her also he learned to keep the vigils of the night in prayer : from her exhortation and example he learned to pray with groanings from the heart and abundance of tears. I confess I marvelled at this great miracle of the mercy of God when I saw such earnestness of devotion in the King, and such sorrow in the heart of a layman when engaged in prayer.

11. A Queen whose life was so venerable, he as it were feared to offend, since he clearly perceived that Christ was truly dwelling in her heart ; he hastened rather the more quickly to obey in all things her wishes and prudent counsels. What she refused he refused, and what she loved, he loved for the love of her love. Hence also the books which she used either in her devotions or for reading, he, though unable to read, used often to handle and examine, and when he heard

from her that one of them was dearer to her than the others,
this he also regarded with kindlier affection, and would kiss
and often fondle it. Sometimes also he would send for the
goldsmith, and instruct him to adorn the volume with gold and
precious stones, and when finished he would carry it to the
Queen as a proof of his devotion. The Queen, on the other
hand, herself the noblest gem of a royal race, made the
splendour of her husband's royal magnificence much more
splendid, and contributed much glory and honour to all the
nobility of the kingdom and their retainers. For she brought
it to pass that merchants who came by land and sea from
divers lands, brought with them for sale many and precious
kinds of merchandise which in Scotland were before unknown,
among which, at the instigation of the Queen, the people
bought garments of various colours, and different kinds of
personal ornaments ; so that from that time they went about
clothed in new costumes of different fashions, from the elegance
of which they might have been supposed to be a new race.
She also appointed a higher class of servants for the King,
that when he walked or rode abroad numerous bodies of them
might accompany him in state ; and this was carried out with
such discipline that wherever they came none of them was
permitted to take anything from anyone by force ; nor did any
of them dare to oppress or injure the country people or the
poor in any way. Moreover, she increased the splendour of the
royal palace, so that not only was it brightened by the different
coloured uniforms worn in it, but the whole house was made
resplendent with gold and silver ; for the vessels in which the
King and nobles of the kingdom were served with food and
drink, were either of gold or silver, or with gold or silver
plated.

12. And this the Queen did not because the honour of the
world delighted her, but because she felt compelled to do what
the royal dignity required of her. For when she walked in
state clad in splendid apparel, as became a Queen, like another
Esther, she in her heart trod all these trappings beneath her
feet, and bore in mind that under the gems and gold there was
nothing but dust and ashes. In a word, in the midst of her

exalted dignity she always took the greatest care to preserve
her lowliness of mind. It was easy for her to repress all swell-
ings of pride arising from worldly glory, inasmuch as the fleet-
ing nature of this frail life never escaped from her thoughts.
For she always remembered the text in which the miserable
condition of human life is described : " Man that is born of
woman, is of few days, and full of trouble. He cometh forth
like a flower, and is cut down, and fleeth also as a shadow
and continueth not." She meditated continually also on that
passage of the Blessed Apostle James, in which he says: "What
is your life? It is even a vapour that appeareth for a little
time, and then vanisheth away." And because as the Scripture
says, " Happy is the man that feareth alway," this venerable
Queen made it the easier for her to avoid sin, as in fear
and trembling she continually kept before her mind's eye the
dreadful day of Judgment. Hence she frequently entreated me
not to hesitate to point out and reprove in private anything
which I saw amiss in her words or actions. Because I did this
less frequently and sharply than she wished, she urged the
duty on me and accused me of being asleep and, as it were,
negligent towards her : "The just man," she said, " shall correct
me in mercy, and shall reprove me ; but let not the oil of the
sinner, that is the flattery, fatten my head ;" for " Better are
the wounds of a friend than the deceitful kisses of an enemy."
She would say this because she sought censure as helping her
advancement in virtue, where another might have regarded it
as a disgrace.

13. This religious and devout Queen, while she thus in mind
and word and deed journeyed on to the heavenly country, also
invited others to accompany her on the undefiled way, in order
that they with her might attain true happiness. The wicked
whom she saw, she admonished to become good ; the good to
be better, and the better to strive to be best. The zeal of
God's house, which is the Church, consumed her so that, aglow
with Apostolic faith, she laboured to root out entirely those
unlawful things which had sprung up within it. For when she
saw that many things were done among the Scottish people
which were contrary to the rule of the right faith and the holy

custom of the universal Church, she appointed frequent councils to be held, in order that by some means or other she might, through the gift of Christ, bring back the wandering into the way of truth. Of these councils, the most important is that in which she alone, with a very few of her friends, for three days combatted the defenders of a perverse custom with the sword of the Spirit, that is, with the Word of God. You would have thought that another Helena was present; for just as she formerly overcame the Jews with the authority of the Scriptures, so now did this Queen those who were in error. At their discussion the King himself was present as an assessor and chief actor, fully prepared to say and do whatever she in this matter might direct. And as he knew the English language quite as well as his own, he was in this Council a most expert watchful interpreter for either side.

14. The Queen opened the proceedings by remarking that all who serve one God in one faith along with the Catholic Church ought not to vary from that Church by new or strange usages. She then pointed out in the first place that they were observing the fast of Lent in a way which was not lawful, inasmuch as they were in the habit of beginning it not with the Holy Catholic Church on the fourth day of the week at the beginning of Lent, but on the Monday of the week following. To this they answered : " The fast which we observe, we keep according to the authority of the Gospel, which states that Christ fasted six weeks." She replied by saying : "In this matter you differ widely from the Gospel, for we read there that the Lord fasted forty days, which you clearly do not do. For when during the six weeks, six Lord's days are deducted from the fast, it is plain that only thirty and six days remain for fasting. Plainly therefore the fast which you keep is not the forty days enjoined by the Gospel, but one of thirty and six days. It remains therefore for you, if you wish to observe an abstinence of forty days, after our Lord's example, to begin to fast with us four days before Quadragesima ; otherwise you alone will be acting contrary to the authority of our Lord, and in opposition to the tradition of the entire Holy Church." Convinced by this clear demonstration of the truth, they

henceforth began the solemnities of the sacred fasts at the same time as Holy Church does everywhere.

15. The Queen also raised another point, and required them to explain for what reason they neglected to receive the Sacrament of the Body and Blood of Christ at Easter according to the custom of the Holy and Apostolic Church. They answered : " The Apostle speaking of those who celebrate the Lord's Supper says : ' He that eateth and drinketh unworthily, eateth and drinketh judgment to himself.' And hence because we acknowledge that we are sinners, we fear to approach that mystery lest we should eat and drink judgment to ourselves." " What ! " said the Queen, " Shall all who are sinners not taste that holy mystery ? No one therefore ought to receive it, for there is not one who is not stained with sin ; not even the infant whose life is but one day on the earth. And if no one ought to receive it, why did the Lord when he proclaimed the Gospel say, ' Except ye shall eat the flesh of the Son of Man, and drink His blood, ye shall not have life in you.' But if you would understand the passage you have adduced from the Apostle in the same way as the Father, it is evident that you must take quite another view of it. For the Apostle does not say that all sinners are unworthy to receive the sacraments of salvation, for after saying, ' he eateth and drinketh judgment to himself,' he adds, ' Not discerning the Body of our Lord,' that is, not distinguishing it in faith from bodily foods, ' he eateth and drinketh judgment to himself.' But he who without confession and penance, and with the defilement of his sins presumes to draw near to the sacred mysteries—he it is, I say, who eats and drinks judgment to himself. But we who many days previously have made confession of our faults, are chastened with penance and fasts, and washed from the stains of our sins by almsgiving and tears—we on the day of the resurrection of the Lord, approaching His Table in the Catholic Faith, receive the Body and Blood of the Immaculate Lamb, Jesus Christ, not to judgment, but to the remission of sins and to the salutary preparation of our souls for the reception of eternal blessedness." To these arguments they could make no

reply, and understanding now the practices of the Church, observed them in the reception of the mystery of salvation.

16. Moreover, there were some in certain parts of Scotland who were wont to celebrate Masses according to I know not what barbarous rite, contrary to the custom of the whole Church. This the Queen, fired by zeal for God, sought to destroy and abolish, so that henceforth throughout the whole of Scotland there was no one who presumed to continue any such practice. It was their custom also to neglect the reverence due to the Lord's Day, and to follow their earthly occupation on that day as on others—a practice she showed them which was forbidden both by reason and authority. "Let us reverence the Lord's Day," she said, "because of the Lord's Resurrection, which took place upon it; let us no longer do servile works on the day on which we know that we were redeemed from the bondage of the devil. This also the Blessed Pope Gregory affirms, saying: 'On the Lord's Day we ought to abstain from earthly labour, and devote ourselves wholly to prayer, in order that if during the six days we have been negligent in anything, we may on the Lord's Day expiate it by prayers.' The same Father, Gregory, after condemning one with the greatest warmth for a certain piece of earthly work which he had done on the Lord's Day, decreed that those on whose advice he had done it should be excommunicated for two months." Unable to contradict these arguments of the wise Queen, they henceforward at her instance observed the Lord's Days with such reverence that no one dared to carry a burden on them, nor did any man venture to compel another to do so. Next she showed how utterly abominable, and to be shunned by the faithful as death itself, was the unlawful marriage of a man with his step-mother, or with the widow of his deceased brother; both of which customs had hitherto prevailed in the country. Many other abuses also which had grown up contrary to the rule of faith and the institutions and observances of the Church, she likewise in this Council succeeded in condemning and expelling from the Kingdom. For whatever she proposed, she so supported with the testimony of the Holy Scriptures and with citations from the holy Fathers, that no one on the

opposite side could say anything at all against it; nay, rather, laying aside their obstinacy and yielding to reason, they willingly undertook to adopt whatever she desired.

CHAPTER III.

Her charity towards the poor.   Her manner of passing Lent.   Her prayerfulness.

THUS the venerable Queen, who by the help of God had endeavoured to cleanse His house from defilements and errors, was found day by day as the Holy Spirit illuminated her heart, more and more meet to become His temple.   And such I well know she truly was, for I both saw the works which she did outwardly, and knew her conscience, for she revealed it to me.   She condescended to converse with me in the most familiar way, and to disclose to me her secret thoughts; not because there was anything good in me, but because she thought there was.   When she conversed with me concerning the salvation of the soul and the sweetness of the life which is eternal, she uttered words so full of all grace that the Holy Spirit, which truly dwelt in her heart, evidently spoke by her lips.   And so deeply was she moved while speaking, that it might have been thought that she would be wholly dissolved in tears, and at her compunction I also was moved to weeping. Beyond all whom I have ever known she devoted herself to prayer and fasting, and to works of mercy and almsgiving. Let me speak first of her prayerfulness.   In a church no one was ever more silent or composed, and in prayer no one was ever more earnest.   For while in the house of God she would never speak of worldly matters, nor do anything which savoured of the earth.   It was her custom there only to pray, in prayer to pour forth her tears.   In the body only was she here on earth; her soul was with God; for besides God and the things which are God's, in her pure supplications she sought nothing.

But what shall I say of her fasting? This only, that by her too great abstinence she brought upon herself a very serious infirmity.

18. To these two, that is, to prayer and fasting, she joined the gifts of mercy. For what could be more compassionate than her heart? What more gentle to the needy? Not only would she give her goods to the poor, but if she could, she would have freely given herself. She was poorer than any of her paupers, for they, having nothing, desired to have, but she was anxious to dispose what she had. When she walked or rode out in public, crowds of poor people, orphans and widows, flocked to her as they would to a most beloved mother, and none of them ever left her without being comforted. And when all she had brought with her for the use of the needy had been distributed, she used to receive from her attendants and the rich who accompanied her their garments and anything else they had with them at the time, to bestow upon the poor, so that no one might ever go away from her in distress. Nor did those who were with her take this ill; they rather strove among themselves to offer her what they had, since they knew for certain that she would pay them the double of what they had given. Now and then she took something or other, whatever it might be, from the King's private property to give to a poor person, and the King always took this pious plundering in good part and pleasantly. On Maundy Thursday and at High Mass he used to make an offering of gold coins, and some of these she would often piously steal and give away to the beggar who was importuning her for alms. Often indeed the King, who was quite aware of what she was doing, though he pretended not to know anything about it, was greatly amused at this kind of theft, and sometimes, when he caught her in the act with the coins in her hand, would jocularly threaten to have her arrested, tried, and condemned. Nor was it to the poor of her own people alone that she exhibited the abundance of her cheerful and open-handed charity, those also were sharers of her bounty whom the fame of her liberality drew towards her from almost every other nation. Of a truth,

to her may be applied the Scripture : " He hath dispersed ; he hath given to the poor ; his righteousness endureth for ever."

19. But who can tell the number of the English of all ranks carried away captive from their own country by the violence of war, and reduced to slavery, whom she restored to liberty by paying their ransom ? She sent secret spies everywhere throughout the provinces of Scotland to ascertain who among the captives were oppressed with the more cruel bondage or were the more inhumanely treated, and to report privately to her where they were and by whom they were ill-treated ; and, commiserating them from the bottom of her heart, she hastened to their assistance, paid their ransom, and restored them to freedom. At that time there were very many in different parts of the kingdom of Scotland who, shut up in separate cells, were leading lives of great strictness, in the flesh but not according to the flesh, for though on this' earth, they were living the life of angels. In these the Queen venerated Christ and loved Him, and frequently occupied herself in visiting and conversing with them, and used to commend herself to their prayers. And since she could not prevail upon them to accept from her any earthly gift, she used to earnestly entreat them to honour her by prescribing for her some work of almsgiving or mercy ; and forthwith this devout woman did whatever they desired, either by rescuing the poor out of their poverty or by relieving the afflicted from the miseries by which they were oppressed.

20. Since the church of St. Andrews was much frequented by the devout, who flocked to it from all sides, she erected dwellings on either shore of the sea which divides Lothian from Scotland, that, after the fatigues' of their journey, pilgrims and the poor might take shelter and rest, and there find already prepared for them all they needed for the refreshment of the body ; for she had appointed servants whose exclusive duty was always to have in readiness everything that these wayfarers might need, and to attend to them with the greatest care. She also provided ships for the transport of these pilgrims, both coming and going ; nor was any toll ever levied from those who were ferried across.

21. As I have spoken of the daily manner of life of this

venerable Queen, and of her daily works of mercy, I will now attempt to give a brief account of how she used to spend the forty days before Christmas and the whole season of Lent. After she had rested a little at the beginning of the night, she went into the church, and there alone she completed first the Matins of the Holy Trinity, next the Matins of the Holy Cross, and then the Matins of Our Lady. When these were ended she began the Offices of the Dead, and after these the Psalter, nor did she cease until she had gone through it. While the priests were saying the Matins and Lauds at the fitting hour, she either finished the Psalter she had begun, or if she had finished it, began it a second time. When she had gone through the office of the Matins and Lauds, she returned to her chamber, and along with the King himself washed the feet of six poor persons, and used to give them something wherewith they might relieve their poverty. It was the Chamberlain's especial duty to bring these poor people in every night before the Queen's arrival, so that she might find them ready when she came to wait upon them. After she had waited upon them, she betook herself to rest and sleep.

22. When the day dawned she rose from bed, and continued for a long time in prayer and reading the Psalms, and whilst reading them performed this work of mercy—nine orphan little children, who were utterly destitute, she caused to be brought in to her at the first hour of the day in order that she might feed them. For she ordered soft food, such as little children delight in, to be prepared for them daily ; and when the little ones were brought to her, she did not think it beneath her to take them on her knee and make little sups for them, and to place them in their mouths with the spoons she herself used. Thus the Queen, who was honoured by all the people, performed for Christ's sake the office of a most devoted servant and mother. To her the words of the Blessed Job might very fittingly be applied : " From my infancy mercy grew up with me, and it came out with me from my mother's womb." While this was going on, it was the custom to bring three hundred poor people into the royal hall, and when they had been seated round it in order, the King and Queen came in, and the doors

were shut by the servants, for with the exception of the chap-
lains, certain religious, and a few attendants, no one was
permitted to witness their alms-givings. The King on the
one side, and the Queen on the other, waited upon Christ in
the person of His poor, and with great devotion served them
with food and drink, which had been specially prepared for
this purpose. When this was finished, the Queen used to go
into the Church and there offer herself a sacrifice to God with
many prayers, sighs, and tears. For besides the Hours of the
Holy Trinity, the Holy Cross, and the Holy Mary, recited
within the space of a day and a night, she would on these holy
days repeat the Psalter twice or thrice, and before the celebration of the Public Mass cause five or six Masses to be sung
privately in her presence.

23. By the time these things were finished, the time for eating was at hand, but before taking her own food she fed
twenty-four poor people, whom she humbly waited upon
herself. For besides the many alms-deeds I have spoken of
already, she supported poor people to this number, that is,
twenty-four, throughout the whole course of the year as long
as she lived. These she desired to live near to wherever
she herself was living, and to accompany her wherever she
went. After she had devoutly waited upon Christ in these,
she used to refresh her own feeble body. In this meal, since
according to the Apostle we ought not to make provision
for the lust of the flesh, she hardly allowed herself the
necessaries of life, for she ate only to sustain life and not to
please her palate. Her light and frugal meal excited rather
than satisfied her hunger. She seemed to taste her food, not
to take it. From this let it be considered, I beseech you, how
great her abstinence was when she fasted, when such was her
abstinence when she feasted. And though her whole life was
one of great temperance, yet during these fasts, that is, during
the forty days preceding Easter and Christmas, the abstinence
with which she was in the habit of afflicting herself was
incredible. Hence, on account of her excessive fasting, she
suffered up to the end of her life from a very acute pain in the
stomach. Nevertheless, her bodily infirmity did not impair

her virtue in good works. Assiduous in reading the sacred Scriptures, instant in prayer, and unceasing in alms-giving, she exercised herself continually and watchfully in all things pertaining to God. And because she knew the Scripture : "Whom the Lord loveth, he chasteneth, and scourgeth every son whom he receiveth," she accepted the pains of her body willingly, and with patience and thanksgiving, as the stripes of a most gracious Father.

24. Since therefore she was devoted to these and similar works, and struggled with her continual infirmities, God's strength, to use the words of the Apostle, was made perfect in her weakness, and going on from strength to strength, she was each day made better. Forsaking in her heart all earthly things, she longed with her whole soul for the things of heaven, yea, thirsted for them, crying out with her heart and voice with the Psalmist : "My soul thirsteth for God, for the living God ; when shall I come and appear before God." Let others admire the tokens of miracles which they see in others, I, for my part, admire much more the works of mercy which I saw in Margaret. Miracles are common to the evil and to the good, but the works of true piety and charity belong to the good alone. The former sometimes indicate holiness, but the latter are holiness itself. Let us, I say, admire in Margaret the things which made her a saint, rather than the miracles, if she did any, which might only have indicated that she was one to men. Let us more worthily admire her as one in whom, because of her devotion to justice, piety, mercy, and love, we see rather the works of the ancient Fathers than their miracles. Nevertheless, it will not be out of place if I here narrate one incident which seems to me to indicate the holiness of her life.

25. She had a book of the Gospels beautifully adorned with jewels and gold, and ornamented with the figures of the four Evangelists, painted and gilt. The capital letters throughout the volume were also resplendent with gold. For this volume she had always a greater affection than she had for any others she was in the habit of reading. It happened that while the person who was carrying it was crossing a ford, he let the vol-

ume, which had been carelessly folded in a wrapper, fall into
the middle of the stream, and, ignorant of what had occurred,
he quietly continued his journey. But when he afterwards
wished to produce the book, he, for the first time, became
aware that he had lost it. It was sought for for a long time,
but was not found. At length it was found at the bottom of
the river, lying open, so that its leaves were kept in constant
motion by the action of the water, and the little coverings of
silk which protected the letters of gold from being injured by
the contact of the leaves, were carried away by the force of the
current. Who would imagine that the book would be worth
anything after what had happened to it ? Who would believe
that even a single letter would have been visible in it? Yet of
a truth it was taken up out of the middle of the river so perfect, uninjured, and free from damage, that it looked as though
it had not even been touched by the water. For the whiteness
of the leaves, and the form of the letters throughout the whole
of the volume remained exactly as they were before it fell into
the river, except that on the margin of the leaves, towards the
edge, some trace of the water could with difficulty be detected.
The book was conveyed to the Queen, and the miracle reported
to her at the same time, and she having given thanks to Christ,
esteemed the volume much more highly than she did before.
Wherefore let others consider what they should think of this,
but as for me I am of opinion that this miracle was wrought
by our Lord because of His love for this venerable Queen.

CHAPTER IV.

The Queen's preparations for her end.   Her sickness and happy death.

MEANTIME, while Almighty God was preparing everlasting
rewards for her works of devotion, she was preparing herself,
with more than her usual carefulness, for entering another life.
For, as her own word a little after showed, it would appear that
her own departure from this life and certain other events were

known to her long before they occurred. Therefore summoning me to come to her privately, she began to recount to me
in order the story of her life, and as she proceeded shed floods
of tears. In short, so great was her compunction while she
conversed with me, and out of her compunction there sprang
such an abundance of tears, that, as it seemed to me, there was,
beyond all doubt, nothing which she might not at that time
have obtained from Christ. As she wept I also wept ; thus
for a time we wept and at times were silent, since by reason
of our sobs we were unable to give utterance to our words.
The flame, as it were, of the compunction which consumed her
heart reached my own soul also, borne into it by the spiritual
fervour of her words. And when I heard the words of the Holy
Ghost speaking by her tongue and clearly perceived her conscience revealed by her words, I judged myself unworthy of
the grace of so great a familiarity.

27. When she had ceased to speak of the things which it was
needful for her to speak, she began to address me again, saying :
" Farewell, I shall not remain long with you in this life ; but
you will survive me for a considerable time. Two things, therefore, I beg of you. One is, that as long as you live you will
remember me in your prayers and at the Mass ; the other is, that
you will take some care of my sons and daughters, pour out
your affection upon them, above all things teach them to fear
and love God, and never cease from instructing them ; and
when you see any of them exalted to the height of earthly
dignity, then at once, as a father or a teacher in the highest
sense, go to him, warn, and when circumstances require it,
censure him, lest, on account of a passing honour, he be puffed
up with pride, or offend God with avarice, or through the prosperity of the world neglect the blessedness of life eternal. These
are the things," she said, " which I ask you, as in the sight
of God who is now present along with us two, to promise me
that you will carefully do." At these words I again burst into
tears and promised her that I would carefully perform what
she had asked me ; for I did not dare to oppose one whom I
heard unhesitatingly predict what was to come to pass. The
truth of her prediction has now been verified by the things

which now are ; since I live and she is dead and I see her offspring raised to dignity and honour. Thus having finished
her conference with me and being about to return home I said
farewell to the Queen for the last time ; for I saw her face no
more.

28. Not long after this she was attacked by an illness more
severe than usual, and was purified by the fire of a tedious
sickness before the day on which she was called away. I will
describe her death as I heard it narrated by her priest, whom,
on account of his simplicity, innocence, and purity, she loved
more intimately than the others, and who after her death gave
himself to Christ in perpetual service for her soul, and having
put on the monk's habit, offered himself as a sacrifice for her
at the tomb of the incorrupt body of the most holy Father
Cuthbert. Towards the end of the Queen's life he was continually with her, and with his prayers commended her soul
to Christ as it was leaving the body. Of her decease as he
saw it he more than once gave me a connected account, for I
often asked him, and he was wont to do so with tears.

29. " For a little more than half a year," he said, " she was
never able to sit on horseback, and seldom to rise from her bed.
On the fourth day before her death, while the King was absent
on an expedition, and at so great a distance that it was impossible for any messenger, however swift he might be, to bring
her tidings of what was happening to him that day, she became
sadder than usual, and said to me as I sat beside her: 'Perhaps
so great a calamity is to-day befalling the realm of Scotland
as has not overtaken it for many ages.' When I heard the
words I did not pay much attention to them ; but a few days
after a messenger came who informed us that the King had
been slain on the very day the Queen had spoken about them.
As if foreseeing the future, she had been very urgent with him
not to go with the army, but it chanced, I know not from what
cause, that he did not follow her advice.

30. " When the fourth day after the King's death approached,
her weakness having abated a little, she went into her oratory
to hear Mass, and there she took care to fortify herself beforehand for her departure, which was already at hand, with the holy

Viaticum of the Body and Blood of the Lord. Refreshed with this health-giving food, she went back to bed, for her former pains returned with greater severity. Towards the end her trouble increases and she was very sorely pressed. What can I do? Why do I delay? As if I were able to defer the death of my Queen, or lengthen her life—thus I fear to come to the end. But 'All flesh is grass, and all the glory thereof as the flower of the grass; the grass withereth and the flower falleth.' Her face had already grown pale with death when she directed that I and other ministers of the sacred Altar with me should stand beside her and commend her soul to Christ with our psalms. Moreover, she requested that a cross should be brought to her, called the Black Cross, which she had always held in the greatest veneration. But as the chest in which it was kept could not be quickly opened, the Queen said with a deep sigh: 'O unhappy that we are! O guilty that we are! Shall we not be permitted one last look of the Holy Cross!' When at length it was taken out of the chest and brought to her, she received it with reverence, and frequently tried to embrace it and kiss it, and to sign her eyes and face with it. Every part of her body was already growing cold, yet as long as the warmth of life throbbed in her breast she continued in prayer. She repeated the whole of the Fiftieth Psalm, and while so doing, placed the Cross before her eyes and held it there with both her hands.

31. 'It was whilst she was doing this that her son, who now after his father holds in this kingdom the helm of the State, arrived from the army and entered the Queen's chamber. What must then have been his distress? What his agony of soul? He stood there in a strait, with everything against him; whither to turn he knew not. He had come to announce to his mother that his father and brother had been slain, and he found his mother, whom he loved most dearly, at the point of death. Whom to lament first he knew not. Yet, the loss of his dearest mother, whom he saw lying almost dead before his eyes, pierced his heart with the sharpest pain. Besides all this, the condition of the kingdom was filling him with the deepest anxiety, for he well knew that disturbances would follow on

the death of his father. On every side he was met by sadness and trouble. The Queen when lying, as it seemed to those present, rapt in agony, suddenly collected her strength and addressed her son. She asked him concerning his father and his brother. He was unwilling to tell her the truth, lest if she heard of their death she herself would immediately die, and answered that they were well. But she, sighing deeply, said : 'I know it, my son ; I know it. By this holy Cross, by the bond of our blood, I adjure thee to tell me the truth.' When he was thus pressed, he told her all as it had happened. What could she do, think you? Who would have believed that in the midst of so many adversities she would not murmur against God? At the same moment she had lost her husband and her son, and a disease had tormented her until she was on the point of death. But in all these things she sinned not with her lips, nor spoke foolishly against God, rather she raised her eyes and hands to heaven and broke forth into praise and thanksgiving, saying : 'Praise and thanks I give to Thee, Almighty God, that Thou hast been pleased that I should endure such great afflictions at my departing, and art pleased, as I trust, that, through enduring these afflictions, I should be cleansed from some stain of sin.'

32. "She now felt that death was close at hand, and at once began the prayer which is wont to be said by the priest after he receives the Body and Blood of our Lord, saying : 'Lord Jesus Christ, who, according to the will of the Father, through the co-operation of the Holy Ghost, hast by Thy death given life to the world, deliver me.' As she was saying the words 'Deliver me,' her soul was delivered from the chains of the body, and departed to Christ, the author of true liberty, whom she had always loved, and by whom she was made a partaker of the happiness of the saints, the example of whose virtues she had followed. With such tranquillity and such quietude was her departure, that there can be no doubt that her soul passed to the land of eternal rest and peace. It was remarkable that her face which, when she was dying, had exhibited the usual pallor of death, was afterwards suffused with red and white tints, so that it might have been believed that she was

not dead but sleeping.   Her corpse was honourably shrouded as became a Queen, and we bore it to the Church of the Holy Trinity, which she herself had built; and there, as she had directed, we committed it to the grave opposite the Altar and the venerable sign of the Holy Cross which she had erected. And thus her body now rests in the place where she was wont to humble herself with vigils, prayers, shedding of tears, and prostrations."

THE LIFE OF S. MAGNUS.

THE LIFE OF S. MAGNUS.

PRAISE, glory, and honour with reverence be unto Almighty God, our Redeemer and Creator, for His manifold goodness and mercy which He has granted unto us, who dwell in the uttermost parts of the earth, and seem to the learned, as they have written in their books, as if we were utterly gone out from the world. Albeit, it has pleased God to show unto us His mercy; especially in this, that he has suffered us to come to the knowledge of His blessed name, and therewith given us strong pillars, most saintly fore-runners of Holy Christianity by whose holiness all the Northern world shines and beams near and far. These are: the King, S. Olaf, and the illustrious Halward, his kinsman, who adorn Norway with their sacred relics; the worthy Magnus, Earl of the Isles, who illumines the Orkneys with his holiness, and to whose honour this history following has been composed. With these are the blessed Bishops, John and Thorlak, who have shed, with holy splendour, their illustrious merits upon Iceland. Wherefore it may be seen that we are not far off from the mercy of God, although our dwellings be placed far from those of other nations; and therefore ought we to give thanks, honour, and reverence all the time of our life.

Master Robert, who has put together this history of the holy Earl Magnus and endited it in Latin, begins his prologue thus, as who will may hear :—

2. Such things as he is able each one brings to the tabernacle of God for help and mercy to himself: one gold, others silver, some precious stones, some goats' hair and red skins of he-goats; and such offerings are not despised; for of such is made the covering for the tabernacle of God, to shelter it and

protect it against moisture and the heat of the sun. These words may thus be glossed with a few words: Let every Christian man offer to God of the gifts and loans which he has granted him, the best he has: so that God's Christianity, which is the tabernacle, which Moses built for the service of God, signifies, that it may serve to defend and strengthen him against the assaults of his enemies. Gold signifies wisdom and knowledge; silver, chastity; precious stones, the miracles of the saints; goats' hair, the repentance of sin; the red skin of the he-goats, martyrdom. Now may the reader observe that all these offerings has S. Magnus offered to his Lord, as the story of his life bears witness. Now, although the praise of God may not be seemly in the mouth of sinful man, still it may be meet and helpful to others; for so we read that the whole house was filled with the sweetest perfume from the ointment and spices of the woman which was a sinner, who in penitence stooped down to wash and anoint the feet of the Lord. But after the wont of the men who till the fields of others but their own neglect and let lie dry, we begin this story of the life of the holy Earl Magnus with the greater confidence and love, and our labour spend upon so holy and noble a narrative, because we trust and fully expect his help to support and strengthen us to his own honour and glory. Now since he is a sharer in the kingdom of heaven and has entered into the kingdom of the Lord, he is able to obtain whatsoever he desires. But since we are sinful and may not, because of our wretched life, set of ourselves good examples to others, we show you the holy Magnus with his glorious life, whom all ought to follow, and take holy example from. Now that we may not be wearisome to the reader with this sermon (for the Lord made short sermons), we shall set forth this story in simple words and in pure speech as God gave us to perceive.

3. In the days of Harold Sigurd's son, King of Norway, there ruled over the Orkneys as Earls, two brothers, Paul and Erlend, the sons of Thorfinn, the most powerful of all the Earls of Orkney. He was son of Earl Sigurd whom King Olaf Tryggvi's son converted, along with all the people of the Orkneys, to the Christian Faith. This Sigurd fell at the

battle of Clontarf in Ireland.   The mother of Erlend and
Paul was Ingibiorg, who was called Earlsmother, the daughter
of Earl Finn Arni's son.   Harold Sigurd's son married Thora,
daughter of Thorberg Arni's son, and mother of Olaf the Quiet,
and therefore third cousins were King Olaf and the aforesaid
Earls.   Earl Erlend married a woman called Thora, daughter
to Summarlid Ospak's son.   Ospak's mother was Thordis,
daughter of Hall of Sida.   Egill was the name of a son of the
aforenamed Hall ; his daughter was Thorgerd, the mother of
S. John, bishop of Holar.   The sons of Earl Erlend and Thora
were S. Magnus and Erling, and daughters, Gunnhild and
Cecilia.   Gunnhild was married afterwards to Kol Kali's son,
a franklin in Norway.   Their son was Rognvald Kali, who
afterwards was Earl in the Orkneys ; he was a very holy man,
and sister's son to Earl Magnus the Saint.   Earl Paul, Erlend's
brother, married a daughter of Earl Hakon, son of Ivar and
Ragnhild, daughter of King Magnus the Good, son of King
Olaf the Holy.   Paul's son was called Hakon, who afterwards
comes into the story.

4.   Earl S. Magnus was born in the Orkneys, the most noble
of race and illustrious of kindred.   His father Erlend was
Earl of Orkney, a worthy lord and ruler, honoured for his
power and greatness, as is the wont of those who live magnificently in this world.   His mother Thora was descended
from the most noble chiefs of this land.   And though with
many greatness of birth is turned to pride and spoiling of
temper, yet was this blessed child already from the earliest
days of his childhood illuminated and instructed by the teaching of the Holy Spirit ; for he held to and loved, honoured
and preserved the highest virtue of the mind, a kindly nature,
and becoming manners, and steadfastness in honourable
ways.   This boy showed himself old in good manners, share-
less in childish life in his deeds, glad spoken aud blithe, gentle
in his loving words, yielding and reasonable in his ways and in
all his behaviour ; well matured and staid, so that nothing was
found in his conduct to anger or offend men who beheld him.
At an early age he was sent to school, to learn the sacred
Scriptures and the other knowledge men then most studied to

know. Magnus was gentle and tractable, docile and obedient
to his father and mother and teachers ; kind and dear to all
the people.   He attached himself little to wickedness and
pastimes as other young men, but conducted himself in a
seemly way, though he was young in the number of his years ;
for there at once shone in him the manifest gift of the Holy
Spirit, which guided him to all good things.

5. While the brothers, Erlend and Paul, held rule in the
Orkneys, there came west from Norway King Harald Sigurd's
son with a mighty army to the Orkneys, and left there
Queen Elizabeth, and Mary and Ingigerd, his daughters. The
earls resolved to accompany the King with a great army, and
held them south to England : and in the battle they fought
with King Harald Godwin's son, fell Harald Sigurd's son, the
fifth night after S. Matthew's day, in the autumn. After this
battle Olaf the Quiet, Harald's son, sailed with the earls that
autumn back to the Orkneys. The same day and the same hour
King Harald fell in England, died suddenly Mary, his daughter,
in the Orkneys ; and the saying is that they had but one life
between them.   Olaf the Quiet passed the winter in the
Orkneys, and was the best of friends with the Earls, his kinsmen, for brother's daughters were Thora, Olaf's mother, and
Ingibiorg, the mother of the Earls. Olaf went in the Spring
east to Norway, and was there made King with Magnus, his
brother.

6. These brothers, Paul and Erlend, ruled the Orkneys a long
time, and long was their agreement good. But when their sons
began to grow up, Hakon and Erling became very overbear-
ing, but Magnus was the quietest and best mannered in every
thing.   All the kinsmen were men of large stature, strong, and
highly accomplished in all things. Hakon, Paul's son, wished
to be overman to Erlend's sons, because he thought he was of
better birth than they ; for he was daughter's son to Earl
Hakon, Ivar's son, and Ragnhild, daughter of King Magnus
the Good, as was before told, and he wished to have a greater
share out of all their dealings. So it came about that they began not to agree ; for many men inclined to Erlend's sons, and
would not have them to be inferior to any in the islands, for they

were of all the people better liked and beloved of men. This was a cause of great offence to Hakon all his life. The sons of the Earls were never safe with each other. Their fathers tried to arrange matters for them, that they might be at peace among themselves. A meeting was called, and it was soon found that each Earl favoured his own sons, and they began not to agree. Then great quarrels arose between these brothers, and so they parted. Next went men between them to make peace, and a meeting was called between them in Hrossey. At this meeting they were reconciled on this condition, that the Islands should be divided into two equal parts; and so things stood for a while. Hakon, Paul's son, greatly molested the men who served Erlend and his sons, so much so that it seemed to them that they could not endure it; and so they began to quarrel, and marched against each other with many men. Havard, Gunni's son, and other chiefs and friends of the Earls then tried to make peace between them, but Erlend and his sons would come to no agreement if Hakon was to remain in the Islands. But as it seemed to their friends that there would be great danger if they were not reconciled to each other, Hakon left the islands at once; and then an agreement was come to between those brothers on the advice of good men. Hakon first went east to Norway to see King Olaf the Quiet; it was towards the end of his days; he dwelt there a short time. Thence went he east to Sweden to see King Ingi, Steinkel's son, and was with him for some time well received. Christianity was then young in Sweden: many men were there who practised the old magic, and thought to become acquainted by it with many things which were not yet come to pass. King Ingi was a good Christian, and took great pains to root out the evils which had long attended heathenism.

7. When Hakon, Paul's son, was in Sweden, he heard tell that there was in the land a man who dealt in divination and spae-craft, whether it was by witchcraft or other means. Hakon was very anxious to meet this man, and to see what he could learn about his fate. He went in search of him and found him in a certain forest country, where he used to go about from feast to feast, and tell the franklins of the seasons and

22

other matters about which they were curious. When Hakon
found this man he inquired of him how it would go with him
for power or other fortune. The soothsayer asked him
who he was. He tells him his name and family, that he
was daughter's son to Earl Hakon, son of Ivar. Then
answers the soothsayer: "Why wilt thou have knowledge or
soothsaying of me? Knowest thou not that thy former kinsmen have had little faith in the kind of men that I am?
And it may serve thy turn to try and learn thy fate from
Olaf the Stout, thy kinsman in Norway, in whom all your faith
is placed. But I suspect he will not stoop to tell thee that
about which thou art curious, or else he is not so powerful as
you call him." Hakon replied : " I will not speak ill of him :
I think rather I am not worthy to get knowledge from him
than that he should not be able to make me wise, if he would.
But I have come to thee because it has come into my mind
that neither of us will have need to look down upon the other
because of virtue or religion." The man answers : " It likes
me well to find that thou thinkest not to have all thy trust in
that in which thy former friends had fait... It is strange also
that the men who seek such things should keep fast and vigil,
and think that thereby it will be given them to know the things
about which they are curious. But though you apply yourselves to such, it turns out that you know less about them as
your curiosity is greater and it is of the greater importance for
you to know them ; but we put ourselves to no pains, and yet
we are able to ascertain the things which it is important for our
friends to know. Now it shall be thus between us two, thou
shalt have this service from me as I see that thou thinkest thyself better able to get the truth from me than from King
Ingi's priests, in whom it seems to him all his trust ought to be
placed. Thou shalt come to me on the third night, we two
shall then see whether I am able to tell thee some of the
things thou art anxious to learn." After this they parted, and
Hakon remained there in the district. And after three nights
he came again to the soothsayer. He was then in a certain
house alone, and breathed heavily when Hakon went in, and
wiped his forehead, and said that he had had to struggle hard

before he became wise in the things he wanted to foreknow.
Hakon replied he would like to know what he had to tell.
He said then : " If thou wouldst know thy fate and about thy
life, it is long to tell : for from thy faring west to Orkney very
great events will come to pass when all the things to which
they lead are fulfilled. And I have a presentiment that thou
wilt become sole ruler of the Orkneys at last, though it
may be that to thee it will seem long to wait. I also think
that thy descendants will remain there. Thou wilt also in thy
days cause a crime to be done for which thou mayest, or mayest
not, get forgiveness from the God in whom thou trustest. But
thy steps lie further out into the world than I can see, yet I
think that thou wilt bring back thy bones to these northern parts.
Now have I told thee the things which at this time I am permitted, but thou wilt decide how thou wilt be content with thy
lot or errand." Hakon answered : " Great things thou tellest
me, if they be true ; but I think it will go better with me, as
it may well be that thou hast not seen these things in their
verity." The spaeman bade him believe what he liked of it.
And on this they parted.

And when Hakon had been a little while with King Ingi,
he fared thence to Norway to see King Magnus Bareleg, his
kinsman ; there he heard tidings from the Orkneys that Earl
Erlend and his sons ruled there most, and were in favour with
all the people, and that Earl Paul, his father, was caring little
about the government. It seemed to him also on inquiry, that
the Orkneymen were longing very little for his own return
home ; they had then good peace, and thought, if Hakon returned, discord and strife would arise. Also it seemed to
Hakon not unlikely that his own kinsmen would keep him out
of the government. He took counsel, therefore, to seek help
from his kinsman, King Magnus, to place him in the government of the Orkneys. Hakon egged on King Magnus greatly
to go a hosting to Scotland and Ireland and then to England
to avenge there King Harald, Sigurd's son. The King answers :
" Thou must bethink, thee, Hakon, if I did this at thy word,
and fared west with an army across the sea, whether it would
not take thee by surprise, if I put forward a strong claim to

those kingdoms beyond the sea, and did it without regarding
the claim of any man." And when Hakon heard this, he grew
cold and was little pleased, but King Magnus ordered a levy
of men and ships over all Norway.

8. Now shall we next turn to the man about whom this history was written, the holy Magnus ; for a little before you have
heard how he was well-behaved in all his conduct and unlike
to other young men in his growing up. But as it is the way with
many to shape their conduct after that of those with whom they
live, and he who touches pitch is defiled by it, so when Magnus
had almost reached the fulness of his growth, placed in the midst
of fierce and wicked men, who were ill-disposed towards good
morals, infirm in faith, opposed to just laws, stiff-necked in
learning, complaisant in evil ways, quarrelsome and disobedient towards the commandments of God, he seemed, for
some winters, to be like wicked men, and as a viking with
robbers or soldiers, he lived by rapine and spoil, and stood by
with others at murders ; and it is credible that he did this more
from the wickedness and egging on of evil men than from his
own badness. It seems likest to men that Magnus did this at
the time when his kinsmen, Hakon and Erling, were all together in the Orkneys, for later no time can be found for it.
Of this conduct, thus speaks Master Robert, who endited this
history :—

" Ah ! I marvel," he says, " how unspeakable is the depth of
the riches of the divine wisdom and of the knowledge of God ;
how unsearchable are his judgments, and his ways past finding
out by human kind. Why permitted Almighty God this His
servant to lust after robbery and murder, and to be defiled with
such manifold sins and misdeeds? Why tholed the divine clemency His knight and martyr to let himself fall so fearfully, who,
from his birth, chose gloriously to crown him in heaven? With
gladness and joy God enriched him, and turned his dust into
heavenly glory, and gave him eternal joy after this world's
sorrow, a garment of beauty and praise after the smitings of
the heart. What is this? unless it be what we daily as openly
as gloriously see, that God raises up and makes sons to
Abraham from stones, just from unjust, honourable from

sinners, glorious from mortal, smooth and polished, and four-cornered, with four main virtues, that they may be made to fit into the heavenly structure, strong and steadfast corner-stones in our chief corner-stone, Jesus Christ, they being of one heart and one mind with Him in the eternal charity and in the bond of infinite love. For the Lord Jesus is the son of the great Builder, who made the earth and all things which are therein, and creates and rules by His own power, and fashions vessels of His wrath into vessels of mercy, polishing them with the file of the Holy Spirit, and He receives sinful men into the widest bosom of His clemency and mercy, all who leave off their foolishness and turn to Him with their whole heart. For it belongs to the great glory and mercy of the Lord to let the abundance of His mercy appear there, where before the burden of our wretchedness was in the way, and he cures and heals the more mightily when the sickness already more fiercely assails the sick man, and makes whole all, and helps those who look to Him for help. See at last how the holy Magnus, though he was entangled in such sins, came to leave off these works and followed his father and brother and the landed men in Orkney."

9. At the time to which we have now come in the story, came west from Norway King Magnus Bareleg with countless ships and many troops. Him followed many of his vassals, Vidkunn Jonsson, Serk of Sogn, Kali of Agde, Saebjörn's son, and Kol, his son, and many other chiefs. The king intended, in this hosting, to subdue and harry the Western lands, England and Ireland, as was before said. When King Magnus came to Orkney, he took the Earls, Erlend and Paul, and drave them out of the islands and sent them East to Norway, and set Sigurd his son over Orkney, and gave him councillors, as he was not older than nine winters. Magnus and Erling, Erlend's sons, and Hakon, Paul's son, he ordered to go with him on the hosting. Magnus, Erlend's son, was tall in stature, bold and fleet and of great strength, of a goodly countenance, fair of complexion, and well shapen in limb, noble in bearing, and most courteous in all his demeanour. Him King Magnus made his table-swain, and he served continually at the King's table. King Magnus fared out of the Orkneys to the Hebrides and subdued in this

expedition all the Hebrides to his rule, and took prisoner Lawman, Gudrod's son, the king of the Hebrides. Thence fared he South to Wales and had there a great fight in the Menai Straits with two Welsh Earls, Hugh the Stout, and Hugh the Brave. But when men picked up their weapons, and got them ready for the fight, Magnus, Erlend's son, sat down in the forepart of the ship, where he was used to sit, and did not arm himself. The king inquired why he did so. S. Magnus answers : " Here I have nothing against any man, and therefore will I not fight." " Go, then," says the king, " below, and lie not here under men's feet, if thou dare not fight, for I do not think thou doest this because of thy religion." Magnus, the Earl's son, sat in the same place, and took a psalter and sang during the battle, but did not shelter himself. The battle was both hard and long. At last fell Hugh the Brave and the Welsh fled ; and King Magnus got the victory, and had lost many good men, and many others were wounded. Kali, Saebjörn's son, received many and great wounds. Magnus, Erlend's son, was not wounded in the fight, though he did not shelter himself. And it might be seen of all, that it was the clearest miracle, that in so thick a flight of arrows, and so heavy a meeting of weapons, he should not be wounded, while on all sides around him fell armed men. And this need not now be wondered at, since God was preserving him for a greater crown and victory than to fall there. King Magnus was not pleased with this, and laid on Magnus, the Earl's son, great feud and dislike on account of it. And when the holy Magnus saw that it would not be for his honour or salvation to remain longer with King Magnus, he took another counsel with himself to do what God taught him.

10. It was one night, when King Magnus lay off Scotland, that Magnus, Erlend's son, stole away from the King's ship, and so arranged his bed, that it seemed as though a man lay there. In the morning, when the King was dressed, he inquired if Magnus, Erlend's son, were sick. He was then inquired for and was missed. The King then let search be made for him, but he was not found. Then the King caused the spoor-hounds to be let loose on the land. Magnus, the Earl's son, had hurt his

foot when he leapt ashore, and the spoor-hounds at once found
the scent. Magnus had made for the woods and climbed up into
a tree. The hounds came to the oak and climbed up into it.
Magnus then struck one of them with a staff he held, and they
immediately took to flight, laid their tails between their legs,
and ran for the ships. Magnus, Erlend's son, hid himself in the
wood while the King's men searched for him. He then fared
up the country and came to the court of Malcolm, King of the
Scots, and dwelt there for a while ; but for some time he was
in Wales with a certain bishop. The same autumn King
Magnus fared back to the Hebrides, and was there through the
winter. That winter died Kali, Saebjörn's son, of his wounds.
Early in spring King Magnus fared to the Orkneys. There
he heard from Norway of the death of the Earls ; Erlend had
died at Nidross and was buried there ; and Paul at Bergen.
Then King Magnus gave Gunnhilda, Earl Erlend's daughter,
the sister of S. Magnus, in marriage to Kol, Kali's son, as an
atonement for the life of his father, with many farms in Orkney. Kol was then made one of the King's vassals. Their son
was Rognvald Kali. Some say that Erling, Erlend's son, and
brother to S. Magnus, fell in the Menai Straits ; but Snorri
Sturlason says he fell in Ulster with King Magnus. For when
King Magnus had ruled nine winters in Norway, he fared west
to Ireland with a great army, and during the following summer
fell in Ulster on Bartholomew's day. And Sigurd, his son,
fared at once out of the Orkneys east to Norway, and was
there made king along with his brothers Eystein and Olaf.

11. You have already heard in a former chapter how
Almighty God is ready to show mercy, whose singular
goodness is always to spare, and to turn hindrances into
helps, and how He preserved this His chosen champion from
the turmoils and dangers of the world, that he might reveal to
him and show how great things it behoved him to suffer
for His name's sake; and he who had often stood among
great manslayers should at length become an offering of the
Holy Spirit, and give to God his own blood with his life and
body. Therefore came he out from the power of the greedy
king, as was before read.

When the holy Magnus was in Scotland, he heard of the death of Earl Erlend, his father, and the other tidings which were before written. And when he had tarried as long in the Scots King's court as pleased him, honoured with the King's gifts and a noble retinue, he fared to Caithness, and there was well received, honoured and esteemed of all, and at once chosen and ennobled with the title of " Earl," beloved and honoured of all the friends of God.

12. Thereafter, without delay, the holy Earl Magnus was made Paul out of Saul, a preacher from a manslayer, and he avenged on himself that which he had lived ill. He began to bewail himself dead in sin with daily moanings and steadfast repentance ; and he now took fitting revenge in manifold inflictions on the sinful lusts of the wretched flesh. He then showed himself a new man, as one who is inclined to that in which God is honoured and whom He has changed into another man, into good from evil, into seemly from sinful, into holy from defiled, into blessed and pure from polluted. This is the conversion of Thy right hand, O Almighty God ! Thou art strong to strengthen, gracious to help, ready to restore, mighty to preserve ! In this way was Magnus changed into a holy man. He began to ear the soil of his heart with the strong ploughshare of confession. Then slew he his man of misfortune and hid him under the sand. Then buried he the graven images of Laban under the roots of the trees. He tore out his sins and pollutions and adorned himself with illustrious virtues in good deeds after a godly manner with manlike steadfastness. He began then to flourish as an olive tree, and to be exalted in all good things and gracious works. Even as a cyprus excels other trees, so S. Magnus grew that he might be truly *magnus* ; i.e., "great" in divine things as he was in name, increasing in prosperity and holiness.

13. A winter or two after King Magnus Bareleg fell, fared from the west over the sea to Norway, Hakon Paul's son, and the kings gave him the title of Earl, and such possessions as stood to him by birth. Fared he then west over the sea and took to himself all the government of the Orkneys, and with such great and aggressive greed that he slew without cause the

steward of the King of Norway, who held and governed that
part of the Islands which the holy Magnus inherited, and in
that way took possession of all the Orkneys by sheer force ;
for half of the Islands belonged to S. Magnus as his patrimony.
Now when the holy Magnus heard with what violence Hakon,
his cousin, had, with manifest injustice, seized his hereditary
lands, he took counsel with his men as to what he should do.
It was agreed among them that he should wait a while, in order
that the anger and greed of Hakon, his kinsman, might abate,
and that it might not appear that he sought his inheritance by
arms, but as a friend and dear lover of law and justice.

14. Now when the time was come that the holy Magnus wished
to visit his patrimony, he fares with a noble company from Caithness to Orkney, and his kinsmen and friends were fain of him.
He asked to take possession of his patrimony.   This was well
pleasing to the franklins ; for he was well loved ; and he had
many kinsmen and connections who were anxious to help him
to hold his dominions.   Thora, his mother, was then married
to a man named Sigurd ; they owned a large farm in Paplay.
When Earl Hakon heard that Magnus was come into the
Islands, he gathered troops around him, and wished not to give
up the government, but to defend it.   Fared then the friends
of both between them, and tried to make peace.   So it came
to pass, through the counsel of good men, that they were reconciled on the condition that Earl Hakon should give up half the
kingdom if it were so decided by the King of Norway. Magnus, Erlend's son, fared at once east to Norway to seek King
Eystein ; for King Sigurd had then fared out to Jerusalem.
King Eystein received the young lord Magnus exceeding well,
and gave up to him his patrimony, the half of Orkney, and
therewith he received the title of Earl in the Orkneys from
the Kings, along with very handsome presents.   And after
this fared the lord Earl Magnus west over the sea to his
dominions, and his friends and kinsmen were glad and with
them all the people.   Then there was much good fellowship
between him and Earl Hakon for many winters, which their
friends brought about.   There was then plenty and peace
in the Orkneys while their friendship held.   The kinsmen,

lord Earl Magnus and Hakon, had both the land defence together for a while, so that they were well agreed. So it was said in the songs, which were made on them, that they fought with the viking called Dufnial, who attacked their kingdom. He was a man one degree further off than first cousin to the Earls, and he fell before them. A man named Thorbjorn, rich and powerful by descent, but poor in good works, they, for sufficient reasons, put to death at Borgarfiord in Shetland. Many other things are also told in songs which they did together, though we cannot here minutely narrate them. The holy Magnus had these things done, not as a viking or robber, but as a just ruler of a province and a guardian of the laws, and a lover of peace, to chastise ill doing and to punish wrong, to make peace and quietness for his subjects and his kingdom against the violence and agression of wicked men, who were always on the watch to break the peace.

15. Lord Magnus was a man the most renowned in his rule and authority, dignified and upright, a steadfast friend and brave, skilled in feats of arms and blessed with victory in battle, gentle in peace, yet a strong ruler, condescending in speech, and clement, prudent in counsel, and had every man's praise. He was open-handed with his money, and generous among chieftains. Every day he gave great help to poor men for the love of God. He punished much harrying and theft, and caused vikings and ill doers, rich as well as poor, to be slain. No respecter of persons was he in his judgments; he respected God's law more than differences of estate among them. In all things he observed strictly the commandments of God, and was unsparing towards himself. Many were the excellent virtues which he manifested before God, but hid from men.

But since the holy Earl Magnus had rule and government over worldly folk, he desired to be like the great ones of the earth in the customs of life; he took and betrothed himself to a high-born princess, and the fairest maiden of the most noble house of the chiefs of Scotland, and brought her home with him and married her. This did the blessed Magnus, as experience proved, with the deep laid counsel of the divine mercy, to impose upon the enticing temptations of this world, rather than to fulfil the lusts of the flesh, for he was helped by divine protection and heavenly power. He dwelt ten years with this virgin, pure and unstained of all the pollutions of sin. And when he felt within himself the temptation to fleshly lust, he plunged into cold water and sought help from God.

16. Behold this strong athlete of God in his daily wrestlings, how wonderfully he lived with this maiden so long a time. For although he lawfully might have enjoyed her, he preferred, sustained by the mercy of the Holy Ghost, to chose the better part, to live inviolate, than to do what is permitted in wedlock, for they suffer the burning of the flesh who do such things. Because better and safer is it to preserve the flowers whole than to restore them after they are bruised; for no wound ever becomes so well as the flesh which has remained whole. But to live in the body without carnal lusts comes not of the power of man, but of the Divine gift. But what temptation and chastening he endured from the lust of the flesh, what heavy blows of forbidden motives, and how hard a struggle he conquered, and calmed the strong lusts of the burning flesh, those know who have experienced them, but the inexperienced believe not. Behold my dearest! This is the great sight which Moses beheld when he saw the bush burning and not consumed; that is to say, this young man was tempted but not overcome. But, as says the Apostle Paul, no one is crowned except he who strives lawfully and works manfully for it, so this prince and wrestling knight preferred Thy courts, to endure the daily conflict and constant battle of the burning flesh. And he fought valiantly and triumphed happily, for it seemed to him that he would be much too easy a knight, who would have glory before he had done works of virtue; for virtue is the way to glory, and glory comes from virtue. Treacherous is the glory, and vain is the beauty which is not begotten by holy virtue. And I marvel, says the Scripture, how fair and winsome is the immaculate conception with its purity and love. This the glorious knight of God, girt with his girdle of chastity, was careful with all mindfulness to do and fulfil all manner of charity to the glory of his Lord. But what of the things of this world would

he deny his God, who expended his very life and body, and
poured out his own blood for the sake of God?

17. Now since no one can be an Abel unless he suffer and
experience the ill-will and malice of Cain, and the holy
Ezekiel dwelt among men full of the poison of adders, and
just Lot was oppressed by unjust men, the enemy of all
mankind stirred up temptations and hot persecutions on every
side against this knight of God, sowing discord and hatred
among brethren and kinsmen and dear friends, all to hinder
him, and to bring to naught his good deeds, which then began
to increase with him ; but the branch of the good vine might
be moved, but not cut off. For as wood swims in water and is
turned over by the winds and waves, but not sunk, and as the
Wain turns round in the heavens, and sinks not, as gold is
purified in the furnace and is not consumed, and as a strong
house is beaten upon by the storms and falls not ; so in the
same way was the mind and heart of this noble martyr strong
and steadfast, undaunted and undismayed amid the fierce
trials and onsets of manifold temptations, in the midst of
storms and great breakers both of secret envy and treachery,
as well as of open ill-will and spite, against the shafts of the
tempting foe. It must next be set down how this discord was
made between the Earls.

18. When the kinsmen, S. Magnus and Earl Hakon, had for
some winters ruled their lands in peace and good agreement, it
came to pass, as it often does, that evil disposed men began to
destroy their brotherly concord. Earl Hakon then drew
towards those evil men, for the kinsmen were very unlike in
temper. Lord Earl Magnus was benevolent and faithful in
his promises ; he wished to retain the kingdom which God had
given to him, and desired nothing more. For in what way
could he be proved to desire other men's kingdoms or possessions, who was so free with his own flesh, that he did not spare
his life for the love of God? He reformed his subjects and
accustomed them to right living, so that after he had delivered
and given peace to his kingdom from the aggressions of wicked
vikings, he did not allow any of his men to go a hosting, and
punished severely all lawlessness and wickedness. But Earl

Hakon was hard-hearted and cruel, greedy both of wealth
and power, and more prone to egg on his men to go a hosting
than to prevent them, and punished little wickedness and
ill-doing. He was very jealous of the liberality and popular
favour of the holy Magnus, and would willingly with the
greed of his evil counsellors overcome the honour of Earl
Magnus, and subdue his kingdom to himself with pillage and
injustice, and began to plot with his men against his life with
treacherous cunning.

19. Now when the blessed Magnus has become thoroughly
aware of this through much experience, which he thinks cannot
be passed over in silence, that Hakon was attempting to deprive
him of his life and kingdom, he took counsel with his counsellors, and it seemed to them that he ought to give way for a
little to the malice and fury of Hakon. Chose he then out of
his people those who were the most suitable and best of his
followers to accompany him, and sailed to England and sought
a meeting with King Henry, son of William the Bastard, who
was then sole king over England. When the holy Magnus
was come to this King, he made known to him the occasion
and object of his coming. And the King received him with
great honour ; and into so great a friendship did he rise with
the King, that he maintained him and all his people at his own
cost for twelve months magnificently, as it was fitting for a
King to treat a famous leader. But this holy martyr held
himself and his retinue so wisely, that he shunned and was
wary of all fellowship with wicked men. And when the lord
King learned from his prudence, how Earl Magnus was a doer
of good works and of seemly manners, and that the Holy Spirit
dwelt in him, he earnestly gave heed to his counsel, and
followed his advice in his conduct, for he was sound and
wholesome in counsel and in making of plans, of
gentle disposition and patient as Chusa, gladsome and loving
as Jonathan, just and zealous for the law as Phinehas. Hence
he was dear to all and beloved, pleasant, and acceptable, so that
there were many who said : " Blessed are they that saw thee,
and that won thy friendship." He was pleasant and kind
to the rich, open-handed and gentle with the poor, good

natured, benevolent, and condescending to all the people.
And although he dwelt at the Court with the princes of this
world, he took care and avoided all kinds of vice which corrupt
the manners of courtiers.   And that he might not for the
future stain his chastity by consenting to other men's sins, he
made ready his home-going as soon as the twelve months
were passed, which he had spent with King Henry.   It may be
that God had made known to him that he should finish his
labours within a short time, and offer to God as well the bright
flowers of his purity as the victorious death of his martyrdom ;
for to be loosed from the body, and to live with Christ, is much
more glorious than to abide here in this polluted world.

20. After that S. Magnus had taken leave of King Henry,
honoured with rich and manifold gifts, and esteemed and
glorified by the Lord King, they parted with the greatest
love and friendship.   He visited first all the holy places which
were near, and then fared home to his own land.   But while
the holy Magnus was abroad, Earl Hakon with great greed and
harrying had subdued not only all the Orkneys, but all Caithness as well, with great robbery and violence ; and so it
came to pass, that Hakon sat at that time in Caithness, when
the holy Earl Magnus landed in the Orkneys with five ships
well manned with valiant and well armed men, ettling to
get back his kingdom, though with no false passion of this
world's ambition, nor greed of unlawful possession, especially
when he had already so long desired God, and was with the joy
of his whole heart wholly taken up out of the lusts of mortal
things into the desire for eternal joy, for he came now to end
his long life into a brief space all the more gloriously the
more quickly he departed.   The tidings of his return home
were at once told on all sides.   Earl Hakon, immediately
awaking as a fierce she-bear robbed of her whelps, summoned and gathered together to him the sons of Belial, cruel ill-
doers, and sons of the wretched Dohet, who always and everywhere wrought evil from their birth from their mother's womb.
Hakon meant then to come unawares upon the holy Magnus,
and to work and complete in that way the malice and treachery
which he had long before had in mind and prepared for.   But

the Supreme Heavenly King, who from eternity had ordained that He would keep His glorious chosen vessel in His treasuries, saw in this man of His own election some rust still of worldly behaviour which required to be purified. Therefore God would that he should be made most pure and fair in a few days with the fire of suffering and insult, and with the files of temptation and of many adversities, though there was no deadly sin in him to wash away. God wished to increase his merit, if in anything it was lacking, that according as his temptation and wrestling were greater and harder, the higher and more splendid should be the glory and joy of the victor. Thus it came to pass that the Earls sent between themselves with messages for peace and reconciliation their most prudent counsellors, who truly bear the marks of Chusa and Ahitophel, who brought about the reconciliation between King David and his son Absolom, when they were at variance. It came then at last in this matter, through the intervention of good men, that a reconciliation was made between the kinsmen in this way, that the earldom of Orkney, Caithness, and Shetland should be divided into halves between the Earls Magnus and Hakon, and that neither should assail the other's kingdom with any greed. When this agreement had been made and confirmed with oaths and handsellings, the Earls met with the kiss of peace. But that which the holy Earl Magnus intended for peace, Hakon turned to deceit and cunning. And the longer he retained the poison of evil, the more wickedly did he spew it up, for his wickedness and villainy increased so much as time went on, that he could no longer hide it. In the same way as a cancer on the face of a man works the more harm the longer it remains, so fares every kind of evil ; thus, the longer it is hid in the mind and heart, the fiercer it becomes for working mischief.

21. The holy Earl Magnus then began again to rule his kingdom with peace and joy for a time. And it is known best in the sight of God how holily he lived in this biding of his death; how he adorned himself with holy virtues and the exercise of every kind of grace, in prayer, and in shedding of tears, and searchings of heart, in purity and nobleness, in alms-giving, and in

all gentleness towards his people, in afflictions and manifold sufferings, which he endured in his body, and in many other virtues more than sinful man can call to mind. As every holy man of God does, in the same way prepared Earl Magnus for his martyrdom; the story of which we shall now with God's help begin.

22. When the above mentioned reconciliation and peace had lasted between the Earls some winters, Hakon showed himself traitorous by pouring out from his breast the great wickedness, which he had for a time held back. Hear how true is that saying of the ancient skald, which says:

> " Nulla fides regni sociis, omnisque potestas,
> Inpatiens consortis erit, totum sitit illa."

That is to say: Never can fellowship in this world's power be true, for no ruler can endure a rival, and would have all to himself alone. From this thou mayest learn what fruit treason begets and what springs up from greed. All sins are done of lust, and every unhallowed desire starts from greed. This is proved by Ahab, that most iniquitous king, who persecuted Elijah the prophet. It is shown by the most wicked Judas, who sold our Lord for money. This same, the traitor, Earl Hakon, showed, both by examples and proofs in the treachery with which he betrayed his kinsman, Earl Magnus, under the show of friendship, though in various ways happened the things which led to their dealings and quarrel.

23. Two men were with Earl Hakon who are mentioned as by far the worst in going between the kinsmen; the one was called Sigurd; the other Sigvat Sokki. Sigurd had a brother, called Thorstein, who was the most faithful follower of Earl Magnus. Many others there were who had an evil hand in this matter, and these were all with Hakon, for S. Magnus would keep no slanderer among his followers. These slanderings went so far that the Earls gathered their troops together, and each fared against the other with a great following. They both held their way to the island of Hrossey, for there was the Thingstead of the Orkneys. And when they were come there, each of them drew up his troops in battle array and prepared

to fight. There had come all the men of rank with the Earls, and many were friends of both, who did everything to reconcile them, and went between them with courage and good-will. This meeting was in Lent. And because many well disposed men were anxious to prevent strife between them, and wished to help neither to do harm to the other, they bound themselves to keep the peace by oaths and handsellings at the witness of the best men. It was settled they should meet in the spring in Egilsey after Easter. At this meeting each Earl was to have two ships and an equal number of men. Both Earls took oaths to have and hold the agreement which the best men should settle at that meeting to declare between them. And after this was done each fared to his own home. With this conditional reconciliation and agreement the holy Magnus was well pleased, as he was thoroughly whole hearted and of good conscience, without all distrust. But Earl Hakon had at this meeting glosed over his treachery and hid it with a cloud of hypocrisy; for this agreement he had made with deceit and treachery and complete fraud, as was afterwards proved ; for at the time Hakon, who is rightly called a treasury of hidden evil, and his wicked servants conspired together in the counsel of their wickedness for the slaughter and death of the holy Magnus. For strong and very dear is all evil amid the fellowship of the scornful ; therefore settled they among themselves that this crime should no longer be delayed, and that now will they fully slake their cruel thirst with the shedding of sackless blood. But the Highest Lord of all power watched over his beloved friend and chosen martyr, that being at this time ready for the kingdom of heaven, he might be taken out of this life under the heavy storm of a violent death ; as grapes under the winepress, trodden upon and crushed, give off the clearest wine in their time with much fragrance and sweet taste, so gave this the glorious martyr of God, by his death, to all the friends of God and his own, the heavenly sweetness of divine mercy, from that glory and joy which he has inherited in the unending gladness of eternal life with God and his saints.

24. As soon as the holy Easter time was passed, each of the two made ready for this meeting in different ways. The holy

Magnus called to him all the men whom he knew had the most good-will to make things better between the kinsmen. He had two longships manned with the bravest men, as many as were agreed upon.   And when he was ready he held to the island of Egilsey. But as they were rowing on a calm sea and in still weather, there rose a wave of the sea beside the ship in which Earl Magnus was, and broke over the place where the Earl was sitting.   The chief men in Earl Magnus's ship were called : Thorstein, who was mentioned before, Arnkell, Grim, and Gilli, and many other doughty men. They marvelled greatly at this circumstance, that the wave fell on them in a calm sea, where no man knew that a wave had fallen before, and where the water under was deep. Then the holy Earl Magnus said : " It is not strange though you wonder at this. But my thought is, that this is a foreboding of the end of my life.   Maybe that will happen here, which was before spaed, that Earl Paul's son will perpetrate the greatest crime : maybe Hakon is plotting treachery against us at this meeting." Earl Magnus's men were much distressed at this speech when he spoke of so speedy expectation of his death, and prayed him to take care of himself and guard his life, and risk nothing to the faith of Earl Hakon.   Earl S. Magnus replies : " I shall certainly go to this meeting, as was agreed upon, and make no breach of my promise for the sake of a mere foreboding. And let all be as God wills about our voyage. But if there be any choice, then would I much rather suffer wrong than do it to another. So may God let Hakon, my kinsman, get forgiveness, though he do me wrong."

Now it is to be told of Earl Hakon, that he called to him a great army. He had seven or eight warships, all of great size, manned with troops ; all the men were well armed as if they were going to battle. But when the force came together, then did Earl Hakon make it clear before his men, that at this meeting it should be so settled with Magnus, that they should not both rule from that time forth.   Many of the Earl's men, who might verily be called children of the devil, expressed delight at this purpose, and added many abominable words ; but Sigurd and Sigvat Sokki were still giving the worst advice ; they were ever egging on to wickedness. The men

then began to row fast, and went furiously and with great
speed. Havard Gunni's son, who was spoken of before, was
with Earl Hakon; he was a close friend of both Earls. Hakon
had hid from him this bad counsel. But as soon as he was
aware of it, he leapt overboard from the Earl's ship and swam
to an uninhabited island; for he would be in no treachery
with Hakon against the holy Magnus. That man was with
Earl Magnus, who was called Holdbodi, a trustworthy franklin
from the Hebrides; he was Earl Magnus's most dear follower.
He was near by all that happened, and has since most clearly
related the dealings and all the discourse of Earls Hakon and
Magnus, which may here be heard next after this.

25. The holy Earl Magnus came sooner to Egilsey with his
men than Hakon. And when they saw Hakon's eight warships, Earl Magnus thought he knew that treachery was being
prepared, and all the men, who had any insight saw well
that such a multitude of armed men was not wanted for a
peaceful purpose. When the holy Earl Magnus saw that the
treachery of Hakon was about to show itself, he went with his
men up into the island to a church to pray, and was there
through the night, not because of fear or dread, but rather to
commit all his care to God. His men offered to defend
him, and fight against Hakon. But he answered: "I will
not place your lives in danger for me. And if peace cannot be made between us two kinsmen, then let it be as God
wills; for rather will I suffer evil and treachery than do it to
others." For this noble martyr, when saying this, knew that
all guile and deceit is returned to him who does it. Now
thought his men most true that which he had before said to
them about the treachery of Hakon. But as Earl Magnus
knew before of his death, whether it were of his foresight or
of divine revelation, he wished neither to fly nor to go far from
the meeting of his enemies, and he went for no other reason to
the holy church than for religion. Earl Magnus watched long
in prayer during the night and meditated on his salvation, and
prayed earnestly; he committed all his cause and himself into
the hands of God. In the morning he let Mass be sung, and
received in that Mass the *Corpus Domini*. And this his deed

was necessary for the highest reason, that in that place he should become an offering to God, as was offered the redeeming sacrifice of the Body and Blood of our Lord Jesus Christ for the salvation of the whole world. But Earl Hakon, who at that time was void of all piety and affection, violating the privileges of the Church, feared not to go into the holy sanctuary, so breaking its peace and immunity, that he might show his wickedness the more fiercely, the more sacred the place he perpetrated it in. For sin is ever increased by ill-doing, and evil by outrage ; and sinful man, when he falls into the depths of sin, abandons all fear of God ; and the more he is acquainted with sin the more he dares, and the less he cares what ill he does ; for he thinks it is nothing worth, however great his misdeeds be. The same morning that Earl Hakon had come up on to the island with his ill-doers, he sent four of his men, the worst of his servants, who were the fiercest and most eager to work ill, to seize Earl Magnus wherever he was. These four, who, from their ferocity, may rather be called the wildest wolves than rational men, always thirsting for bloodshed, leapt into the church just as Mass was ending. Snatched they at once the holy Earl Magnus with great violence, uproar, and clamour, out of the peace and bosom of Holy Church, as the gentlest sheep of the fold.* The Saint was holden of the thralls of sin, the righteous was bound, dragged unjustly by the unjust, and then led away before the greedy judge, Earl Hakon. But this strong champion had such great steadfastness in all these wrestlings, that neither his body shook from fear, nor his mind from dread or grief, for he forsook this thorny world with all its fruitless flowers. He hoped that God would recompense his patience

---

* The Shorter Saga gives a different account. " Next morning he went out of the Church with two men out on the island down to the shore to a certain hiding-place, and prayed there before God. Some men say that Earl Magnus caused mass to be said for him before he went out from the Church and that he took the *Corpus Domini*. Earl Hakon and his men ran up on the island in the morning, and first to the church, and sought for Earl Magnus, and did not find him there. Then they searched for him about the island. But when Earl Magnus saw where they were, he called to them and said " Here I am." And when Hakon saw that, they ran thither. Cc. 11, 12.

with an ineffable crown ; but their cruelty and fury with everlasting torture in the hot fire of hell, because of their inhuman
wickedness and monstrous greed.   He was as glad and cheerful when they took him, as if he had been bidden to a banquet,
and had so settled a heart and mind that he spoke to his
enemies with no bitterness, anger, or tremor in his voice.

26. When the holy Earl Magnus was come before Earl
Hakon, he said to Hakon with great calmness : " Not well doest
thou, kinsman, when thou kept not thy oath, and it is much
to be looked for that thou didst this more from the malice and
egging on of others than from thine own ill-will.   Now I will
make to thee three offers, that thou mayest take one of them
rather than that thou shouldst break thy oath, and let me thy
kinsman be slain, sackless as some will say." Earl Hakon said:
" I will first hear what thou offerest."   S. Magnus said : " This
is the first offer, that I shall fare abroad to Rome or all out
to Jerusalem, to seek the holy places, and so make atonement
for both of us ; I will take two ships out of the land furnished
with good men and the equipment needful to have.   I will
swear never to come to Orkney again."   This offer was
quickly refused by Hakon and his men.   Then said Earl
Magnus : " Now since our life is in your power, and I know
that in many things I have offended against Almighty God,
and have need thereof to make amends, send me up to Scotland
to the friends of us both, and let me there be in ward with two
men with me for amusement ; and see thou so to it that I may
never come forth of that wardship without thy leave."   This
they at once rejected and found many reasons why it could not
be.   Then spake this doughty knight : " Now is my choice very
limited, says he.   Now is there but one choice left, which I will
offer thee, and God knows that I am more concerned for thy
salvation here, than for the life of my body ; for, after all, it
beseems thee little to take my life.   Let me be maimed in my
limbs, or let my eyes be put out, and set me so in a dark
dungeon, whence I may never come out."   Then said Earl
Hakon : " This offer take I, and no more do I ask."   Then
leapt up Earl Hakon's men and said : " In this finding we
do not agree, to torture Earl Magnus : but one or the other of

you two we will slay; and from this day you shall not both of
you reign over these lands." Then says Earl Hakon: "Rather
will I rule the lands than die at once, if ye are so strict in this
matter." So tells Holdbodi of their parley.—After this S.
Magnus fell to prayers and bowed his face into his hands and
shed many tears before God, giving his cause, his life, and himself, into the power of the Lord.

27. Next to this, when the holy friend of God, Earl Magnus,
was condemned and doomed to death, Earl Hakon bade Ofeig,
his standard-bearer, slay Earl Magnus; but he refused with
greatest anger. Then compelled Earl Hakon his cook, who
was called Lifolf, to smite Earl Magnus, but he began to weep
aloud. Then said Earl S. Magnus to him : "Weep not; for
there is fame to thee in doing the like. Be thou of steadfast
mind, for thou shalt have my clothes as is the wont and law
of the men of old. Thou shalt not be afraid, for thou doest
this by force, and he that forces thee to it has more sin
than thou." And when he had said this, he took off his
kirtle and gave it to Lifolf. Then begged the blessed Earl
Magnus leave to pray first, and it was granted him. He fell
then to the ground and gave himself into the power of God,
offering himself to Him in sacrifice. Not alone for himself prayed
he, but rather for his enemies and murderers as well ; and
forgave he them all with his whole heart that which they were
misdoing against him ; and confessed he all his sins to God,
and prayed that they might all be washed away by the shedding of his blood ; and he commended his spirit into the hands
of God, praying God's angels to come to meet it, and bear
it to the rest of Paradise. Then when this noble martyr
of God had ended his prayer, he said to Lifolf : "Stand before
me and hew me on the head a great wound ; for it beseems
not to behead chiefs like thieves. Be strong, man, and weep not,
for I have prayed God to pardon thee." After this Earl Magnus
crossed himself, and bowed him to the stroke. Lifolf struck
him on the head a great blow with an axe. Then said Earl
Hakon : "Strike again." Then struck Lifolf into the same
wound. Then fell the holy Earl Magnus on his knees, and
fared with this martyrdom from the miseries of this world to the

everlasting joys of the kingdom of heaven. And him whom the murderer took out of the earth, Almighty God let reign with Him in heaven. His body fell to the earth, but his spirit was gloriously taken up into the heavenly glory of the angels. The spot where the holy Earl Magnus was slain was stony and mossy. But a little after his merits before God were made manifest, so that since then there is there a green field, fair and smooth, and God showed by this token, that Earl Magnus was slain for righteousness sake, and gained the fairness and greenness of Paradise in the land of the living.—The death-day of the holy Earl Magnus is two nights after the feast of Tiburtius and Valerianus ; it was on the second day of the week, that the worthy Earl Magnus was slain, the third week after Lady Day in Lent. He had then been twelve winters Earl with Hakon. Then were Kings in Norway Sigurd the Crusader, and his brothers Eystein and Olaf. Then had passed from the death of the holy Olaf, Harald's son, seventy-four years [eighty-six]. It was in the days of Pope Paschal, the second of that name, and of S. John Bishop of Holar in Iceland.—In honour of the holy Earl Magnus thus speaks Master Robert who in Latin this history endited :

28. "To-day shines upon us, dearest brethren, the day of the death of the blessed Earl Magnus the Martyr, the day of his rest and of his eternal joy. Let us be glad and rejoice on this glorious day ; for he requires of us solemn devotion and especial thanksgiving, who live beside his holy relics and under his protection and keeping, and have hope in his merits. For it was on account of his noble example and holy life that first flourished in the coasts of the kingdom of the Orkneys the seemly ordinances of pure devotion, and the most holy laws of this most glorious martyr brought forth manifold fruit in good living. He drave abroad the lordly throne of Satan out from the northern regions of the world and set in its place the tabernacle of Almighty God. He laid waste and uprooted all the tares by his preaching, and let spring up the fairest flowers and the sweetest harvest of most life-giving fruit. He turned all the bitterness of the Orkneys into praise and sweetness of holy living. On this day he overcame the

world and the princes of the world, and he went up, a radiant
conqueror over the world, receiving from his holy Master, our
Lord Jesus Christ, a crown of glory.   On this day he was
set free from all bondage of fleshly corruption, entering into
heaven ; and he went into joy, made like the saints in all
glory.   On this day he laid aside the earthly garments of this
changeful life, and went up higher than human weakness may
reckon ; and on him therefore is bestowed greatness in heaven,
honour and blessedness in the presence of all the saints.   He
ascended radiant according to his merits, rich in the fulness of blessing, glorious in noble victories.   This glorious
martyr of God, the blessed Earl Magnus, adorned with the
crown of his own blood, suffered after the incarnation of our
Lord Jesus Christ, one thousand one hundred and four [six-
teen] years, on Monday the sixteenth of the kalends of May.
Now it remains, my dearest brethren, that we lay aside fleshly
lusts and beware of loving unlawful things, vanquishing and
overcoming the assaults of sin, and follow the footsteps and
life of this glorious martyr with all the strength of our mind as
far as our weakness will allow.   Let us follow the way of his
life ; let us hold to the example of his works.   Let us strive to
make our lives like his, though it daily appeareth and is
shown forth—by those wonderful tokens and glorious works
which Almighty God doth grant unto the North both by sea
and land for the sake of his excellent prayers and famous
merits—that his life and holy righteousness are things more
meet for us to honour and wonder at than to be imitated
by our weakness.   He appeared on earth, that he might become
our protector and ask help and grace for us from Almighty
God.   Therefore it behoves us, who are pressed down under the
great load of our sins, honour always to do to him with the
especial goodness of bounden obedience and honour, that this
glorious martyr, Earl Magnus, may vouchsafe to obtain for us,
by means of his merits and prayers, that we may win to become sharers of his victorious crown and eternal glory, which
he won on the day of his passion.   This grant us the Lord
Jesus Christ, who is the honour and blessing, the help and salvation, the gladness and glory of all His holy and righteous men ;

who with the Father and Holy Ghost liveth and reigneth, One God in Three Persons, world without end. Amen."

Master Robert wrote this history in Latin to the worship and honour of the holy Magnus, Earl of the Isles, when twenty years were gone from his passion.

29. Now must we take up the story again, and tell of the things which were done after the death of the holy Earl Magnus. So great was the fierceness and cruelty of Earl Hakon, and so great his anger and fury at the blessed Magnus, that he bore not less malice to Earl Magnus dead than living. And though the anger and fury of most men can be abated after the doing of their ill deed, the ill will and malice in the heart of Hakon took no rest and abated not ; for he forbade Earl Magnus to be buried at the Church as Christian men, but ordered that he should be hidden there in the ground where he was slain.

30. It had been agreed at the first meeting of the Earls in Hrossey, that when their reconciliation had been fully made and confirmed as the best men determined, as they had bound themselves by oaths, that both Earls, when they fared from the meeting, which was fixed to be held in Egilsey, should go to a feast in Paplay at Thora's, the mother of Earl Magnus. But now, after the slaying and death of the Earl, went Earl Hakon to the banquet with his men. The feast was of the best. Now when drink took hold on Earl Hakon, then went Thora to him and spake thus: "Now art thou come here alone, lord ; but I expected both of you, thee and Earl Magnus my son. Now be thou so to my prayer as thou wilt that Almighty God shall be to thee at doomsday ; that thou grant to me that my son may be buried at church." Earl Hakon looked on her, and shed tears, and said : " Bury thy son, woman, where it likes thee." Earl S. Magnus was then borne to the church, and buried in Birsay, at Christ's Kirk, which Earl Thorfinn, his grandfather, let be built. Immediately a heavenly light was often seen to shine over his grave. Then men began to call upon the holy Earl Magnus, when they were placed in danger, and he met their need as they prayed. Always was a heavenly odour perceived at his grave, and there sick men obtained health.

Next, sick men made journeys from Orkney and Shetland, who were hopeless of cure, and watched before his tomb, and were cured of all their diseases, but still men did not dare to make known the miracles of Earl Magnus while Earl Hakon lived. So it is told, that the men who had been worst between the Earls and most in treachery towards Earl Magnus, came most of them to speedy ends and short life, and died a shameful death.

After the death of Magnus, Hakon, Paul's son, took possession of all the Earldom of the Orkneys. He compelled all men to swear oath and fealty to himself, as well those who before had served Earl Magnus. He became great, and laid heavy burdens on the friends of Earl Magnus, whom he thought had been most against himself in their negotiations. Some winters after, Hakon made ready to go abroad. He went south to Rome, and on that journey went all the way to Jerusalem, as was then the custom for palmers. He sought the holy places, and bathed in the river Jordan. After that he returned to his own land and took up the government in the Orkneys. He became then a good ruler, and established good peace in his kingdom. He made new laws, which the franklins liked much better than those which had been before. By such things he began to increase his popularity. So it came to pass that the people of the Orkneys would have no other than Earl Hakon and his offspring to hold rule among them. And here is the end of what is to be said about Hakon in this book.

31. The most merciful God, our Lord Jesus Christ, who invites and leads His friends to everlasting joy, from all the bondage of this world, . . . the same who redeems all who humble themselves to His mercy, with their whole heart, from all the sins and pollutions of this sorrowful world, and makes of the ignorant the wisest, of the lowly and despised the most famous, of the poor the richest, of the ignoble the noblest rulers, not only of the kingdoms of this world, but also of the kingdom of heaven, and of eternal glory, as He did aforetime with the patriarch Joseph, who was led out of a dark dungeon and at once made prince and ruler over all the land of Egypt : the

same who made of the shepherd boy, David, the greatest king over all the tribes of Israel, and led Judas Maccabæus out of the famine of the desert, that he might obtain honour and the renown of victory, and so great a fame that in many things he is thought to far excel others, and Alexander, the son of Philip, who was called the Macedonian, because of the hard mastership of Aristotle *   .   .   .   .   .   .

15. At this time William was bishop in the Orkneys. Then was the bishop's seat at Christ's Kirk in Birsay where the holy Earl ·Magnus was buried ; he doubted long about his holiness and kept down this new thing [*i.e.*, the miraculous virtue experienced at the grave of S. Magnus, c. 30.]

16. Bergfinn, Starri's son was the name of a franklin north in Shetland. He was sightless, and fared south to the Orkneys and watched at the tomb of the Earl S. Magnus. With him watched two men, one was named Sigurd and the other Thorbjorn ; they were both cripples. Earl S. Magnus appeared to them all and made them quite cured. Again twenty-four men watched at the tomb of Earl Magnus and all got healing for their hurts.

Many men told this before Bishop William and urged him to speak about it with Paul, Hakon's son, who then ruled over the Isles after his father, and ask him to give leave that the sacred relics of Earl Magnus might be taken up out of the ground, but the bishop took that heavily. Often was he reminded in dreams that he should make up his mind about the Earl's holiness, and yet he would not believe in it. Afterwards it so came about that he was beaten with divine scourges that he might honour the tokens and holiness of Earl Magnus.

17. One summer Bishop William sailed East to Norway on some pressing business, and immediately turned homewards in the autumn, and came in the beginning of winter to Shetland. There he was laid up by contrary winds and storms. But when for a long time during the winter there was no fair

---

* The following paragraphs are taken from the Lesser Saga in order to fill up the gap which occurs here in the Greater Saga.

wind for the isles, the Bishop despaired of being able to reach his see before spring. The captain asked him if he would agree to the holiness of Earl Magnus if he should sing mass the next Lord's Day at home. The bishop, so to say, gave his consent to this, but more from necessity than of free promise. But when this was agreed, there was calm weather and soon a fair wind. And afterwards they sailed for Orkney ; and he came home also before the next Lord's Day ; and all praised God and also his holy martyr Earl Magnus. Some men say this, that Bishop William did not agree to take out of the ground the sacred relics of Earl Magnus before it happened there at home one day at a time that he could not get out of the church. For he had become blind and could not find the door, till he repented of his unbelief, and wept bitterly, and besought God that he might light upon the tomb of Earl Magnus. And when he came there, he fell all his length on the ground, and promised to at once take out of the earth his sacred relics, when he received his sight. And when he had ended his prayer, he received his sight there at the tomb.

18. Afterwards he summoned the wisest and the best men in Orkney, and there came a great multitude to Christ's Kirk at Birsay. Then were taken out of the ground the sacred relics of Earl Magnus, and then the bones were almost come up out of the ground. He then let wash the bones, and the joint of the finger to be taken and tested in the consecrated fire thrice. But it burnt not, rather it became like burned silver. Some men said it ran into the form of a cross. Then there were many miracles done by the holy relics. After that took learned men the holy relics and laid them in a shrine, and set them over the altar. That was on Lucy's day [December 13] before Yule; and then there had passed twenty years since the slaying of Earl Magnus. The day of his death is holden in spring, the sixteenth of the kalends of May [April 16]. Bishop William directed the festival to be held on either of the two days over all his bishopric ; and he was afterwards in great love with the holy Earl Magnus. William was the first bishop in Orkney, and ruled sixty-six years.

* . . and prepared in every respect as becomingly as possible. Then enshrined the lord Bishop the holy relics of the blessed Earl Magnus with honour and reverence and the hymns of all the people, and there were healed all who were lacking health, and in need of pity, who at that time had thither sought his sacred relics. Earl S. Magnus was enshrined on the Feast of the Virgin Lucy, before Yule in the winter. And that day is widely held in veneration both for the holy Magnus and God's blessed Virgin Lucy, but in Spring is his home-faring day to the kingdom of heaven.

32. Now was before told, though less fitly than briefly, about the uptaking, probation, and enshrinement of the sacred relics of the blessed Earl Magnus, and not less of the fixing of his festival. And it is to be remembered and recorded that with sundry privileges does the Lord God honour his beloved friends because of their righteousness, some here immediately in this life, but others after life. Yet seem those dignities among the saints, somewhat special and surpassing, which belong to God's martyr Magnus. That is to say, that when his bone was proved at home in the Orkneys, it turned into the most beautiful cross in the eyes of the men who were present. Of this same is another example, that this same bone-cross was afterwards turned into the most brilliant gold colour even before the Lord Pope himself at Rome. Wherefore he receives this purple martyr into the Catalogue of Saints; but that has been granted to few others in these Northern lands, that he himself [the Pope] has done this. Therefore may we behold and wonder, though none may conceive it as it is, how abundant is God Almighty in His riches and in the depths of His mercy: for He grants these gifts of love to some of His friends, which He grants not to others, and divides them among them as He wills ; and He fails none, though He gives the gifts of the Holy Spirit to each of them. Therefore be His name ever praised and blessed throughout the ages. Amen.

33. From that time were spread abroad and celebrated the miracles of the holy Earl Magnus over all the western and

---

* The narrative of the Greater Saga is here resumed.

northern parts of the world, and men fared from neighbouring lands, burghs and towns, castles and districts, with great hearts and offering hands, to seek his holy relics, and some sent presents to his sacred shrine, to his honour but for their own healing and salvation, both in this world and in the next. Therefore shall here be told some miracles, though but a few, from the countless number which God granted because of his merits :—

34. When Bergfinn, the franklin north in Shetland, who was named before in this history, heard the joyful tidings of the translation of the holy Earl Magnus, he fared a second time south from Shetland with his leprous son, named Halfdan, to Kirkwall ; and watched, both father and son, at the sacred relics of Earl Magnus. And the holy man of God appeared to Halfdan and passed his hands over his body and at once fell from him all his leprosy. Then he rose up healed. Earl S. Magnus also appeared to the franklin Bergfinn in a dream and said to him : "Now shalt thou receive clear sight, for hither hast thou now come with a true faith and didst not distrust my sanctity, and didst offer to me fair vows, both in prayers and offerings." Then he made the sign of the Cross over Bergfinn's eyes ; and he awaked seeing as well as when he had been sharpest sighted. And father and son both fared home healed, praising God and the holy Earl Magnus.

A man, hight Thorkell, who dwelt in the Orkneys, fell off his barley-rick and was maimed all over one side when he came to the ground. He was borne to the holy Earl Magnus and received there the speedy healing of his hurt, so that his broken bones grew together again and his body was made strong. He thanked God and the holy Earl Magnus for his healing gift.

A man, called Amundi, son of Illugi, a franklin north in Shetland, was a leper and very sick. He fared to the holy Earl Magnus and watched at his shrine and prayed for mercy and healing. As he slept Magnus Earl of the Isles appeared to him and passed his hands over his body and gave him so speedy a cure that he awoke quite whole ; and gave he to God thanks for his healing and to the gracious Magnus.

A man, hight Sigurd, Tandri's son, dwelt in Shetland at
the farm called Dale. He became mad, so that he was sewn
up in hide. This man was carried to the holy Earl Magnus
and got there his senses and complete health, and fared thence
sound and whole, praising God and the holy Earl Magnus.

Another man, also hight Sigurd, north in Shetland, had his
hands so twisted that all the fingers lay in the palm. He
sought the sacred relics of the holy Earl Magnus and received
there healing, with straightness and suppleness of his fingers
for all his needs. Thanked he God for the mercy which He
had granted him for the merits of Earl Magnus.

A man called Thorbiorn Olaf's son, north in Shetland,
was witless and possessed of a devil. He was taken to the
place of the holy Earl Magnus, and was there at once made
whole, and fared back to his house rejoicing and praising God
and this blessed martyr.

Thord, who was surnamed Dreka-Skolptr (Dragon-Snout),
was hireling to the aforenamed franklin Bergfinn. He was
threshing corn in the barley barn on the day before the mass-
day of the holy Earl Magnus. But about 3 o'clock in the
afternoon Bergfinn bade him leave off work. "It is very
seldom," said Thord, "that it seems to thee that too much has
been done." Bergfinn said: "The festival which falls to-
morrow ought to be kept with all the honour we may and
can." Bergfinn then went away, but Thord worked on as before. When a little while was passed, Bergfinn went out again
and said to Thord in great anger: "It is the greatest offence
to me that thou workest at holy times. Leave off at once on
the spot." The franklin went away very wroth, but Thord went
on working as before. But when men had nearly done eating,
in came Thord in his working clothes and began at once to
drink greedily. When he had drunk one horn of ale, he became
mad, so that the men had at once to bind him with bonds and
that continued for six days. Then the franklin Bergfinn promised
for him to give half a mark of silver at the shrine of the holy
Earl Magnus, and to let Thord watch there three nights if he
might be made whole. Thord was at once healed the next
night after the promise had been made for him. And all praised

the Highest King of Heaven and his beloved friend the holy Earl Magnus.

It is also said that two men broke gold off from the shrine of the holy Earl Magnus ; one was a Caithness man, the other an Orkneyman. He of Caithness was lost and drowned in the Pentland Firth, and was hight Gilli. The Orkneyman went mad and told in his ravings what they had done. Then was a promise made for him of a pilgrimage to Rome if he were made whole. Afterwards he was taken to the holy Earl Magnus, and a vow was made to him for his recovery, and he became whole at once, and praised God and the holy Earl Magnus.

There was a man called Asmund. On his head fell a great tree and broke all his skull, but the oft-named franklin Bergfinn made a vow for him ; and lots were cast whether there should be promised for him a pilgrimage to Rome or an offering to the Church of Magnus. And the lot came up that he should visit the sacred relics of the holy Earl Magnus. He obtained at once the use of his tongue which he had before lost. He fared then after that to the holy Earl Magnus and watched there and obtained a complete cure of all his hurts. And the franklin Bergfinn gave to Earl Magnus half a mark of silver weighed as he had promised.

There was a woman called Sigrid ; she was the daughter of Sigurd of Sand north in Shetland. She was blind from tender babyhood until she was twenty. Her father took her south to Orkney and let her watch at the shrine of Earl S. Magnus. He offered there a great present. Sigrid received then clear sight in both eyes, and they fared thence, father and daughter, rejoicing and praising God and the holy Earl Magnus.

There was another woman also called Sigrid, daughter of Arnfrid, from the farmstead called Unst north in Shetland. Her leg was broken in twain, and she was taken to the holy Earl Magnus ; and was quickly cured, and thanked God and the holy Earl Magnus.

A third woman also called Sigrid from Unst north in Shetland, was working with the franklin hight Thorlak who lived at Bollastede (Batlasta). Sigrid was sewing in the evening before the mass-day of the holy Earl Magnus after others were keeping the festival. Thorlak enquired why she worked so long, and she answered she would stop. The franklin went out, but she sewed as before. Then came Thorlak again to her and said : " Why doest thou so wrongly at so holy a time ? Now go away and work no longer in my house." She made light of the offence, and then went on sewing as before till it was dark night. But when the men were getting ready to eat, Sigrid became mad so that she had at once to be put in bonds and was grievously possessed, till Thorlak made a promise for her and lots were cast, whether she should fare to Rome or give goods to Earl Magnus. And the lot was thrown that she should go to Kirkwall to the sacred relics of the holy Earl Magnus. Afterwards she was taken thither and got there a wonderful gift of healing of her madness ; and she praised God and his exalted knight Earl Magnus, nevertheless she afterwards fared to Rome for her salvation.

A woman called Groa, from Hrossey, was possessed by an evil spirit and fared to Kirkwall to the holy Earl Magnus, and got there a good cure, and praised God and the holy Earl Magnus.

There was a woman named Ragnhild ; she became a cripple when she was four winters old and all up till she was twenty, then watched she three nights at the holy relics of the Earl S. Magnus. On the third night there appeared to her in her sleep a man bright and glorious, and splendidly clad, and said to her : " Long and often hast thou lain here, great is thy need, rise up now and be made whole and take this staff in thine hand." After that he vanished from her. But she wakened ; she was then holding on to the lock that was on the aumbry on the other side of the Magnus choir. Rose she then up at once completely healed, as if she had never been crippled, with sound bones and sinews, praising God and the holy Earl Magnus. She was with the bishop many winters.

Asa was the name of a woman who had all her days been a cripple. She obtained so excellent a cure from the blessed

Earl Magnus, that she went to Rome that same summer she was healed.

Gudrun was the name of a woman ; she was a cripple for a long time. She obtained a speedy cure of her maimness and a complete cure through the merit and intercession of the holy Earl Magnus, and praised God and his beloved Earl Magnus.

There was a man called Sigurd. He was alms-man at Knot-Sand. He was so very decrepit that he crept on his knees and could not stand upright. He was cured at the shrine of Earl Magnus. He praised God and the holy Magnus.

Two Southerners cast dice for money—one lost a hundred marks. Then was lost all his wealth, except one cog he had left. He then staked the cog against every thing he had lost. Then he who won before, threw two sixes. But for his help the other made a vow to the holy Earl Magnus, that he might get back the rest of his property. After that he threw, and turned up six on one dice, but the other sprang asunder in two parts, and there were seven spots on the two together and thirteen on the three ; and so he won back all his wealth.

35. It happened in Norway, in the days of Harold Gilli, that some rich men and distinguished gave out that two brothers intended to beguile their kinswomen. But the accusation was not true. All the same, the two rich men attacked them, and took them captive, carrying them away from others into a wood, and slew the one of whom they had the greater suspicion. Afterwards they took the other and gave him many and hard tortures with much cruelty, insomuch that they brake in sunder both his legs and as well his arms. After this these cruel men put out both his eyes, therewith cutting his tongue away out of his head, and in such inhuman wise leaving him, they went away ; but he lay there half dead. As soon as they were away, leapt out from the woods many wolves, riving and tearing the flesh from the bones of him who was slain, faring after back into the wood. But of him who was wounded it is to be told that though he could not pray with his tongue for pity, he continually bethought him that Almighty God would grant him some help. Especially did his mind turn there where the holy Earl Magnus was, for at that time

was flourishing most of all his miracle-working. And when
he had made a vow, he became aware that a man was come
to him who was stroking his broken arms and legs. Therewith he takes the short part of his tongue and brings it to
its place at last ; he then lays his hand on the sockets of his
eyes. And with this handling came a wonderful change ; the
eyes took their places with clear vision, the tongue immediately becomes framed for all kinds of speech, the broken
limbs were healed, and all his former health restored. He
sees standing by him a man of fair countenance, with whom
he spake, saying : " What is thy name, noble lord ? " The
resplendent man answers : " Here is Earl Magnus, but take
good heed to perform that which thou hast promised to the
Lord." At this he became joyful, and spake thus to him again :
" Since, exalted friend of God, thou hast granted to me a great
gift of healing, I beseech also of thy clemency to intercede with
God for my brother's life." After he had thus spoken, the holy
Magnus vanished away from his sight without answering to
his prayer. But he fell down and thanked God for the mercy
vouchsafed to himself, intending to bide in that place two
nights in steadfast prayer for the help of his brother. And as
the time wore on he looks round, and sees a great pack of
wolves run from the wood to where the corpse lay, and spew
up there all they had eaten of his flesh and bones, and turn
again to the wood. And when a little time was passed, he
sees S. Magnus come, and bless with his right hand all the
wolves' vomit and the bones ; then next to this the body becomes all sound. S. Magnus blesses again his lifeless body,
wherefore he rises up whole and living who before was slain,
and goes to his brother. Greeted then each of them the
other, giving thanks to God and the holy Magnus for so marvellous a mercy as had been granted them. So also let all
hearing such miracles, give manifold praise to the true God,
who grants such wonderful things to sinful men because of
the prayers and merits of his own best beloved friends.

19.* There was a trusty franklin in Westray, called Gunni.
He dreamt that the holy Earl Magnus came to him and said :

---

* This and the following chapters are from the Lesser Saga.

"This shalt thou say to Bishop William, that I would fare out of Birsay east to Kirkwall, and I trust that God will there grant me of His mercy that those who seek me there with a true faith may be healed of their pains. Thou shalt tell thy dream boldly." But when he awoke, he did not dare to tell the dream, because he feared the wrath of Earl Paul. The following night Earl Magnus appeared to him and bade him tell the dream when many were by : " But if thou dost not do so, thou shalt suffer punishment in this world and more in the next." And when he awoke he was filled with fear and fared to Hrossey to see the bishop, and tells the dream at the bishop's mass in a great crowd of men. Earl Paul was there, and all the people prayed the bishop to bear the sacred relics to Kirkwall as Earl Magnus had shown. But Earl Paul stood by silent, and turned blood red. After that fared Bishop William east to Kirkwall with a noble retinue and bore thither the sacred relics of Earl Magnus. The shrine was set over the altar in the Church which is there. There was then at Kirkwall but a trading village with few houses, but it has since greatly increased. Many men have since fared thither and watched there in the Church at the holy relics and have been healed if they vowed to Earl Magnus with true faith.

20. When Earl Rognvald Kali, sister's son to Earl S. Magnus, had come to rule in the Orkneys, and was quietly seated, he caused the ground-plan of the Magnus Church in Kirkwall to be marked out, and got workmen for it, and the work went on well and swiftly ; and it is a noble work and well finished. Afterwards were the sacred relics of Earl Magnus flitted thither, and many signs were wrought there at his holy relics. There is now also a bishop's see which was before at Christ's Kirk in Birsay.

A man, called Eldjarn, the son of Vardi, had a wife and many children, and lived north in Kelduhverf. But during a bad season he became poor and sick, so that he could not help himself, and so little strength had he that he was unable to walk and was driven about among the homesteads. It fell after Easter in spring that he had been driven about on Thursday, Friday, and Saturday, and had had no food. He came at nones

on Saturday to where the priest lived and was there through
the night. In the morning when men fared to matins, he
prayed that he might be taken to the Church; and it was
done. After the matins men fared indoors between the services.
But he lay out of doors there where his bed was made : he was
so feeble that he thought he was about to die. It came also
into his mind how he had been before his poverty when he had
his property all together, and his prayer which he prayed,
touched him so much that he was greatly moved. Then he
took and promised a six days' fast, if God would give him some
relief : this fast he vowed both before S. Olaf's and S. Magnus'
day. When he had uttered his vow, men came to the service
and the priest sang mass. When the Epistle was read he fell
asleep, but those who were beside him thought he was about
to die. In his sleep a vision passed before him, in which he
thought he saw a great light within the choir, and that it came
out to him. He saw with the light a beautiful man, and he
said to him : " Eldjarn ! hast thou little strength now ? " He
thought he answered : " So methinks, though perhaps it may
not be so. But who art thou ? " He answers : " I am Earl S.
Magnus, Erlend's son. Wilt thou be made whole ? " He
answers : " I will." He replied : " King S. Olaf also has heard
thy prayer and the vow which thou hast made to us two for
thy healing. But he sent me hither to give thee healing : for
a woman made a vow to him west in the Firths, and he has
fared thither to make her whole." Then began Earl Magnus
to pass his hands over him, but he woke up when the Gospel
was begun. He asked the men who stood nearest him to lift
him up. But they answered : " Why should we lift thee up,
when thou hast no strength ? " He replies : " I think I am
now cured." They took him and raised him on to his feet, and
he stood all through the Gospel and so on to the end of the
mass. After mass he went in to the priest and tells the miracle,
how God had given him healing. And all praised God for the
mercy which He had granted to him for the merit of Earl S.
Magnus. May he obtain for us mercy and pardon for our
sins from our Lord Jesus Christ, who, with the Father and the
Holy Spirit, liveth and reigneth God for ever and ever. Amen.

INDEX.

INDEX.

	PAGE
Ached-bou,	108
Aethne, mother of S. Columba,	53
Aid the Black,	83
Aid, son of Ainmurech,	94
Aid, King,	66, 67
Aidan, King,	33, 65, 149
Aid Slane,	68
Aidan, son of Fergno,	76
Ailbine, Delvine,	100
Ainmire, son of Setna, King,	64
Airtheara, Kings of,	89
Airthrago, island of,	143
Ait-Chambas Art-Muirchol,	115
Alva,	291
Aporic Lake, the,	128
Artbranan,	81
Ard Ceannachte,	101
Ardnamurchan,	67
Artur, son of Aidan,	65, 66
Baitan, of Lathreginden,	72
Bede, the Venerable, his statements as to SS. Ninian and Columba,	5
Berach,	71
Berchan, surnamed Mesloen,	162
Boend, river,	104
Bos, river,	88
Brecan, whirlpool of,	107
Breg, plain of,	86
Brenden Mocualti,	76
Brito, a monk,	150
Broichan, the Druid,	124, 125
Brude, King,	55, 124, 126
Brude, King, son of Dagart,	289
Cailtan,	79
Campulus Bovis,	108
Candida Casa,	11
Catlon, King, defeated and slain by Oswald,	57
Cellrois, monastery of,	89
Cethirn, fortress and well of,	94
Christ's Kirk, Birsay, burial of S. Magnus, 353; enshrinement of his relics,	356,357
Clochur,	102
Clonifinchoil, monastery of,	169
Cnoc Angel,	158

	PAGE
Cogreth, lake,	92
Coire Salchain,	92
Colga, son of Aid Draigniche,	70
Colga, son of Cellach,	82, 103, 157
Colonsay, island of,	87, 115
Colman, the Hound,	89
Columb, a blacksmith,	153
Cooldrevny, battle of,	53, 64
Congal, abbot,	94
Conall, bishop of Coleraine,	95
Connal, King,	64
Cronan, bishop,	90
Cronan, the poet,	88
Culross,	187,289
Cuuleilne, in Iona,	84
Daire Calgaich,	134
Dairmaig (Durrow),	61, 95, 99
Deathrib, great cell of,	96
Deisuit, her sight restored by S. Ninian,	27
Delvin, the river,	101
Dermit, King (Aid Slane),	68
Diormit, King,	82
Diormit, S. Columba's servant, 42, 44, 65, 67, 74, 76, 78, 81, 96, 121, 122, 166
Diuni, a monk,	79
Domingart, son of Aidan,	65, 66
Domnall, son of Aid,	66
Domnail, son of Mac Erca,	65
Druids,	55, 106, 124
Druim Ceatt,	66, 103
Drumalban,	81
Drumpelder, hill of,	184
Dunning,	292
Dysart,	289
Echoid, Bude,	66
Echoid Find, son of Aidan,	65, 66
Echoid Laib,	65
Edgar, King,	300
Edmund, King,	298
Eigg, island of,	160
Eilean-na-naiomh, 33, 37, 91, 117, 149, 159, 160
Elgu, the river,	229
Elne plain of,	95
Emchath,	156

PAGE

Erco Mocudruidi, a thief,......... 87
Erland, Earl in the Orkneys, 326; his sons quarrel with Hakon, Earl Paul's son, 328; driven from the Orkneys to Norway by Magnus Bareleg, 333; dies at Nidross, 335
Ernan,................................ 69
Ernan, uncle of S. Columba,.... 91
Ernene, son of Crasen,............ 61
Failbhe, Abbot of Iona,........... 57
Farres Last,......................... 18
Fechna, a penitent,................. 78
Fedilmith, father of S. Columba, 53
Feradach, ... 116
Field of the Two Streams, monastery of,........................... 128
Finten, son of Aid,................. 122
Forcus, son of Mac Erea,......... 65
Ford Clied, Dublin,............... 101
Gallan, son of Fachtna,.......... 82
Gemman, ... 118
Germanus, Bishop,............... 126
Glasderc,............................ 69
Gore, son of Aidan,......... 92
Hakon, Earl, son of Earl Paul, 327; his pride, 328; molests the sons of Earl Erlend, 329; goes to Norway, *ibid.*; consults a spaeman, *ibid.*; visits Magnus Bareleg, 331; receives his patrimony from the Kings of Norway and the title of Earl, 336; seizes the whole Earldom of the Orkneys and slays the King's steward, *ibid.*; on the arrival of Magnus comes to an agreement with him, 337; a quarrel fomented between him and Magnus, 340; seizes the whole Earldom and Caithness, 342; agreement with Magnus, 343; another quarrel fomented between him and Magnus, 344; they meet at Hrossey, *ibid.*, and agree to meet at Egilsey after Easter, 345; their meeting there, 349; the slaying of Magnus, 350; goes to the house of Thora, who begs of him the body of Magnus, her son, 353; rules the Earldom, 354; makes a pilgrimage to the Rome, Jerusalem and the Jordan, in which he bathes, *ibid.*; his rule,.......................... *ibid.*
Harald, Sigurd's son,............. 328

Holdbodi, ... 347
Hynba (Eilean-na-Naoimh), 33, 37, 73, 91, 112, 117, 159, 160, 170
Ictean Sea, ... 288
Inchkeith, island of, ... 288
Indairthir, Anterii,.............. ... 151
Iogenan, ... 105
Iona, island of, 69, 71, 72, 87, 120, 131, 155, 157, 163, 171, 264
Islay, isle of,......................... 116
Jocelin, Bishop of Glasgow,...... 177
John, son of Conall, ... 115
Kinel,................................. 288
Kernach (Carnoch),.............. 199
Laisran Mocumoie, the gardener, 71
Laisran, son of Feradach,......... 67, 78
Laloecen,............................. 279
Lam-dess, ... 117
Langueth, Queen, ... 256
Lea, district of....................... 74
Ledon, the river,................. 199
Libran of the Rush-ground,...... 131
Lifolf,................................ 350
Lothweiverd, ... 270
Lough Key,............... ...... 88, 112
Lugaid, surnamed Laitir,......... 130
Lugbe Mocumiu, messenger of S. Columba,... 69, 75, 77, 87, 119
Lugne, a pilot, ... 137
Lugne Mocublai,.................... 157
Lugne Mocumin,.................... 119
Lugucencalad, ... 106
Lugud Clodus,...................... 86
Lunge, plain of,..................... 88, 109
Magnus Bareleg, is visited by Hakon, 331; visits the Orkneys with a fleet, compels Earls Paul and Erlend to go to Norway and their sons to accompany him on his expedition south, 333; subdues the Hebrides and overcomes Hugh the Stout and Hugh the Brave, 334; returns to the Orkneys and Norway, 335; his death,.. .... *ibid.*
Malcolm, son of Duncan, King, 301
Mallena, the river,................. 197
Manus Dextera,.................... 117
Maugina, daughter of Daimen, 102
Maugdorn, district of,............. 89
Mayonius, Bishop of Alexandria, 284
Melconde Galganu,................. 231
Meldan,.............................. 69
Mellindenor, Molindenar,........ 265
Miathi, battle of, ... 65
Monglas, ... 288
Morken, King of Cambria, 221, 223, 225

PAGE

Morthec, ... 279
Muirbolc Paradisi,................... 67
Mull, island of,..................... 87
Munhu (S. Kentigern),............ 194
Munitio Magna,...................... 100
Neman, son of Gruthrich, ... 86
Ness, the river........................ 119
Nigra Dea, river of,................ 129
Oingus, son of Aid Comman,.... 68
Oissene, son of Ernan,............. 61
Ommon, island of, ... 83
Ondemone, battle of,.............. 64
Oswald, King, his vision, 46,
  56 ; made Bretwalda,........ 57
Paul, Earl, in the Orkneys, 326 ;
  his sons quarrel with those
  of Earl Erlend, 328 ; is com-
  pelled to leave the Orkneys
  for Norway by Magnus Bare-
  leg, 333 ; dies at Bergen,... 335
Pertnech, Patrick,.................. 279
Picts, Northern,.................... 55
Picts, Southern, converted by
  S. Ninian, ... 15
Pilu, a Saxon,...................... 163
Pons Servani,....................... 197
Plague, the,........................ 144
Rechrea, island of,................ 137
Rederech, 244, 247, 250, 256, 260, 278
Roderc, son of Tothal, King of
  Alcluith, 69. See Rederech.
Robert, Master,............ 325, 351, 353
Rognvald Kali, 335 ; founds the
  Magnus Church at Kirkwall, 304
Ronan, son of Aid,................. 89
S. Adamnan, his reasons for
  writing the life of S. Col-
  umba, 51 ; meets Servanus,
  288 ; is visited by him,...... 289
S. Ailred complains of the man-
  ners of his age, ... 19
S. Asaph,..................... 232,246
S. Baithene, Abbot of Iona, 59,
  72, 74, 84, 109, 152, 160
S. Brendan, of Birr, his death
  revealed to S. Columba, 34,
  154 ; sees an angel accompanying him,.................. 147
S. Cainnech, Abbot of Ached-
  bou, ... 63, 108
S. Ceran of Clonmacnoise,....... 61
S. Colman, in danger in the
  whirlpool of Brecan, ... 63
S. Columba, his Life by Cui-
  mene the Fair, 31-47 ; his
  nativity, 31, 147* ; a globe
  of fire appears over his face,
  32, 147 ; he has an angel

PAGE

  for his companion, ibid.,
  148 ; turns water into wine,
  ibid. ; is shown the glass book
  of the ordination of Kings,
  consecrates Aidan king, and
  foretells future things concerning his son, 33, 149 ; sees
  a monk received up into
  heaven, 34, 150 ; has the
  death of S. Brendan revealed
  to him, also the death of S.
  Columban, 35, 155 ; he fights
  with demons, ibid., 152 ; by
  means of an angel renders
  help to a monk in Ireland
  though himself in Iona, 36,
  157 ; he converses with angels, 37, 157 ; a ball of fire
  is seen to rise from his head,
  ibid., 159 ; enjoys celestial
  visions during three days, 38,
  160 ; relieves a poor man,
  ibid.; is suffused with heavenly light, 39, 161, 162 ;
  his life is prolonged, 40, 164 ;
  he predicts his own death,
  41, 164; sees an angel, ibid.,
  165 ; indicates the hour of
  his death, 42, 166 ; his occupation just before his death,
  ibid., 168 ; his last words,
  43, 168 ; dies in the Church,
  ibid., 169 ; burial, 44 ; the
  storm during his obsequies,
  45, 171 ; various miracles,
  ibid.; a miracle wrought by
  his tunic, 47, 147 ; a prediction concerning Ernene,
  son of Crasen,.................. ibid.
Life by S. Adamnan, 51-174 ;
  meaning of his name, 52 ;
  his birth predicted by Maucta, ibid.; his parentage and
  childhood, 53 ; his miracles,
  55 ; a prophecy he uttered
  concerning S. Fintan, son of
  Tailchan, 60 ; Ernene, son
  of Crasen, 61 ; the speedy
  arrival of S. Cainnech, 63 ;
  prays for the safety of bishop
  Colman, ibid. ; prophesies
  concerning Cormac, 64 ;
  foretells the issue of the
  battle between King Ainmire
  and the two sons of Mac
  Erca, Domnel and Forcus,
  ibid.; also of the battle of
  the Miathi, 65 ; prophecies

* The second numbers refer to the same incidents in S. Adamnan's Life.

PAGE

concerning the sons of Aidan, *ibid.,;* Domnal, son of Aid, 66; Scandlan, son of Colman, *ibid.;* Baitan and Echoid, 67; Oingus, 68; Aid Slane, *ibid. ;* King Roderc, 69; two boys, *ibid.;* Colga, son of Aid Draigniche, 70; Laisran, the gardener, *ibid.;* a great whale, 71; a certain Baitan, 72; one Neman, 73; one guilty of incest, *ibid.;* the vowel I, 75; a book, *ibid.;* his inkhorn, *ibid.;* the arrival of a guest, 76; a man calling out from the other side of the Straits, *ibid.;* a Roman city, 77; a vision concerning Laisran, son of Feradach, 78; prophecies concerning a penitent, *ibid.;* his monk Cailtan, 79; two brothers. 80; Artbranan, 81; a fire, *ibid.;* Gallan, son of Fachtna, 82; Findchan, 82; the consolation he sent to his wearied monks, 83; his voice, 85; he chants evensong before the gates of King Brude, *ibid.;* prophecies concerning Lugud Clodus, 86; Neman, son of Gruthrich, *ibid.;* a priest in Trioit, 87; the thief Erco Mocudruidi, *ibid,;* the poet Cronan, 88; two noblemen, 89; he recognises in a visitor a bishop, 90; prophecies concerning Ernan, the priest, 91; a peasant, 92; Gore, son of Aidan, *ibid.;* a crane, 93; the fortress of the Cethirn and its well, 94; certain presents, 96; he turns water into wine, 98; makes the bitter fruit of a tree sweet, 99; causes corn sown after midsummer to be reaped in August, *ibid.;* by blessing water cures many, 100; water into which a box he had blessed was dipped heals Maugina, 102; the cure of divers diseases at the Ridge of Ceatt, 103; salt blessed by the Saint cannot be consumed by fire, *ibid.;* a book written by him is not destroyed by water, 104; a similar miracle, *ibid.;* water

PAGE

caused to flow from a hard rock, 105; a prophecy concerning Lugucencalad, 106; the water of another fountain sweetened, *ibid. ;* he stills a tempest, 107; his prayers rescue Cainnech, *ibid.;* the miracle of Cainnech's staff, 108; he gives prosperous winds to Baithene and Columban though sailing in different directions, 109; drives a demon out of a milk-pail, 110; he discovers and brings to naught the works of a sorcerer, 111; heals Lugne Mocumin, 112; miracle of the salmon, *ibid.;* he indicates where two fish will be found, *ibid.;* increases the herd of Nesan, and prophesies the minishing of Uigene's, 113; multiplies the number of Columban's cows, 114; prophesies the death of John, son of Conall, who had despised him, 115; also of Feradach, 116; of Manus Dextra, 117; of another oppressor of the innocent, 118; slays a wild boar with his word, 119; drives back an aquatic monster in the river Ness, *ibid. ;* drives poisonous reptiles out of Iona, 120; blesses a knife so that it will hurt neither man nor beast, 121; cures Diormit, 122; Finten, son of Aid, *ibid.;* raises a dead boy to life, 123; causes the Druid Broichan to be seized with sickness, and a captive maiden to be set free, 124; he overcomes Broichan, 126; causes the gates of King Brude's fortress to open, 127; also the doors of a church, *ibid.;* provides for a poor peasant by blessing a stake, 128; predicts that the flowing tide will bring back a milk-skin which the ebb had taken away, 130; his prophecy concerning Libran, 131; his prayer brings help to a woman in child-birth, 139; he reconciles Tutida and his wife, 137; his prophecy respecting Cormac,

PAGE

grandson of Lethan, 139; his prayers change the directions of the winds, 142; and protect against the plague, 144; the apparition of angels which S. Brendán saw about him, 147; he sees angels carrying the soul of the blacksmith Columb to heaven, 153; the soul of a woman, *ibid.*; sees angels meet the soul of S. Brenden of Birr, 154; also the soul of S. Comgell, *ibid.*; and the soul of Emchath, 156; he sees angels coming to meet his own soul, 163; a white pack horse places its head in his bosom and seems to bemoan the Saint's approaching end, 167; his death revealed to Lugud, son of Tailchan, 169; to Ernene, 170; his twelve companions, 173; his parents and relatives, ... *ibid.*

S. Columba visits Kentigern,.. 264

S. Columban, death revealed, ... 35

S. Comgel, ... 95

S. Cormac, grandson of Lethan, 64, 138

S. David, ... 226, 229, 235

S. Fernaus sees S. Columba surrounded with heavenly light, 39

S. Findchan, founder of Artchain, Tiree, ... 82

S. Findbarr (Vinnian), bishop, a teacher of S. Columba, ... 98

S. Finnian sees an angel accompanying S. Columba, 32; celebrates Mass when water drawn by S. Columba is turned into wine, ... *ibid.*

S. Finnio, a teacher of S. Columba, sees an angel accompanying him, ... 148

S. Fintan, Abbot, son of Tailchan, S. Columba's prophecy concerning him, ... 58

S. Kentigern, conception, 179; birth, 184; education, 187; is falsely accused and restores a bird to life, 189; kindles fire by breathing upon a hazel bough, 191; raises the dead cook to life, 194; leaves S. Serf, 196; visits Fregus at Carnoch, 199; blesses Anguen, 201; the punishment of Telleyr, 202; election and consecration as bis-

PAGE

hop at Glasgow, 203; his example and doctrine, 206; his dress, 207; couch, vigils and bath, *ibid.*; his mode of speaking, 209; is adorned while celebrating Mass, *ibid.*; how he spent Lent, 211; the brightness of his countenance, and his opinion of hypocrites, 214; he converts and edifies the people, 216; yokes a stag and a wolf together in a plough, and, sowing sand, reaps wheat, 218; uses the force of the Clyde to confute Morken, 221; is struck by Morken, 223; withdraws to Wales, 226; meets S. David, 227, and Cathwallain, 228; led by a white boar to the spot he builds a monastery on the banks of the Elgu, 229; is opposed by Melconde Galganu, 231; number of brethren in the monastery, 233; sees S. David crowned in heaven, 235; his prediction concerning Britain, 236; visits to Rome, 237; Pope Gregory confirms his election, 240; the character of two clerics revealed to him, *ibid.*; divine vengeance overtakes his adversaries, 242; is invited back to Strathclyde by King Rederech, 244; leaves S. Asaph to govern the monastery and sets out for Cambria, 246; his reception and and works, 248; is honoured by King Rederech, 250; his zeal, success and miracles, 252; the miraculous protection of his clothes, 254; he restores to the Queen her ring, which had been thrown into the Clyde, 256; he provides fresh mulberries after Christmas, 260; milk turned into cheese when spilled into the river, 263; is visited by S. Columba, 264; he relieves and converts certain thieves who had killed one of his sheep, the head of which stuck to the hands of him who had seized it, and had been turned to stone, 267; he erects crosses

PAGE

in various places, 268; he
prepares for death, 271; his
disciples desire to die with
him, 273; the manner of his
death, 275; his burial,...... 279
S. Margaret, her descent and
virtues, 298; marriage, 301;
builds the Church of the
Holy Trinity at Dumferm-
line, *ibid.;* presents a mag-
nificent cross to the Church
at St. Andrews, 302; her
chamber like the workshop
of a heavenly artificer, *ibid.;*
the women she employed,
ibid.; her care for her children, 303; for the honour
of the kingdom, 304; the
King's devotion to her, and
her influence over him, *ibid.;*
encourages trade, 305; her
influence over the Court,
ibid.; reforms the Church,
306; her charity, manner of
passing Lent, and prayer-
fulness, 310; redeems captives, 312; places vessels
for the conveyance of pilgrims across the Forth, *ibid.;*
her copy of the Gospels is
miraculously preserved, 315;
her preparations for death,
316; her last illness and
death, 318; her burial,...... 321
S. Martin of Tours visited by
S. Ninian, ... 10
S. Maucta, prediction concerning
S. Columba, ... 51
S. Ninian, his birth, 6; parentage, baptism and education,
7; his arrival at Rome, 8;
his studies there, 9; is sent
by the Pope to Britain,
ibid.; visits S. Martin of
Tours, 10; desires masons
of him, *ibid.;* builds the
Church of S. Martin at
Whithorn, 11; heals and
converts King Tudvallus,
ibid.; vindicates an innocent
presbyter, 13; undertakes
the conversion of the Southern Picts, 15; his miracle
among the leeks, 16; he
protects certain cattle, 17;
restores a thief to life, 18;
is protected when reading
against the rain, 20; why
on one occasion he was not,
20; a miracle wrought by

PAGE

his staff, *ibid.;* the miracles
wrought by his relics,........ 25-28
S. Servanus (Serf),.............178, 191
S. Servanus, his conception, 283;
baptism and education, 284;
ordination, *ibid.;* elected
bishop of the Canaanites,
ibid.; patriarch of Jerusalem,
285; resides at Constantinople, 286; visits the island
of Salvatoris, *ibid.;* elected
to the Chair of S. Peter at
Rome, *ibid.;* leaves Rome,
ibid.; ascends the Alps, 287;
he and his company are assailed in the Valley of Beasts,
ibid.; crosses the Ictean Sea,
288; meets S. Adamnan,
ibid.; arrives at Kinel, *ibid.;*
takes up his abode at Culross, 289; is opposed by
Brude, son of Dagart, *ibid.;*
builds a church, *ibid.;* visits
Adamnan in the island of
Leven, *ibid.;* restores a brother in the cave at Dysart,
ibid.; his controversy with
the Devil in the same cave.
290; cures a man of an evil
spirit at Tillicoultry, 291; a
miracle performed at Alva,
ibid.; slays the dragon in the
Dragon's Den at Dunning,
292; is visited by three men
from the Alps whom he
heals, *ibid.;* his death and
burial at Culross,.......... ... 293
Salvatoris, island of,.............. 286
Saxonia,............................ 66
Scandlan, son of Colman,........ 66
Seghine, Abbot of Iona,.......... 57, 62
Sigurd, one of Hakon's retainers, 344
Sigvat Sokki, one of Hakon's
retainers, ... 344
Silnan, a monk,...................... 87, 100
Skye, isle of,........................ 81, 119
Snam-luthir, monastery of, ... 141
Snorri Sturlason,.................... 335
Suibne, son of Columban,........ 68
S. Magnus, his parentage, 326;
early virtues, 327; youth and
conduct, 332; is compelled
to accompany Magnus Bare-
leg, and is made his table
swain, 333; his conduct dur-
ing the battle in the Menai
Straits, 334; he escapes from
Magnus Bareleg, *ibid.;* visits
the Court of Malcolm Can-
more, 335, and a certain bis-

PAGE

hop in Wales, *ibid.;* goes to Caithness and receives the title of Earl, 336; his austerities, *ibid.;* goes to the Orkneys and comes to an agreement with Hakon, 337; the agreement confirmed by the King of Norway, *ibid.;* his character as a ruler, 338; a quarrel fomented between him and Hakon, 340; he visits the English Court, 341; his return to the North, 342; reconciliation of Hakon, 343; another quarrel fomented between him and Hakon, 344; they meet at Hrossey, *ibid.,* and agree to meet at Egilsey after Easter, 345; their meeting there, 346; his death, 350; his burial in Christ's Kirk, Birsay, 353; sick men healed at his grave, *ibid.;*

PA(

enshrinement of his relics, 356, 357; canonisation, 357; his miracles, 355, 358, *et seq.;* translation of his relics to Kirkwall, ... 36
Taneu, mother of S. Kentigern, 179, 18
Tarain, ... 11
Tauri Vestigium, ... 1.
Tillicoultry, ... 29
Tiree, island of, ... 71, 72, 10(
Tomma, Ridge of, ... 17(
Trena, a monk, ... 7(
Triot, monastery of, ... 8;
Tudvallus, his conversion by S. Ninian, ... 11
Valley of Beasts, ... 287
Virgnous, Abbot, ... 161
William, Bishop of the Orkneys, refuses to believe in the miracles wrought at the grave of S. Magnus, and how he is brought to honour him, ...355, 356